JOINT HEIRS
WITH CHRIST

McDougal & Associates
*Servants of Christ and Stewards of
the Mysteries of God*

JOINT HEIRS
WITH CHRIST

by

Dr. Abiola Idowu

JOINT HEIRS WITH CHRIST
Copyright © 2025—Abiola Idowu
ALL RIGHTS RESERVED

Published by:

McDougal & Associates
www.ThePublishedWord.com

McDougal & Associates is dedicated to spreading the Gospel of the Lord Jesus Christ to as many people as possible in the shortest time possible.

ISBN: 978-1-964665-30-6

Printed on demand in the U.S., the U.K., and Australia
For Worldwide Distribution

DEDICATION

This book dedicated to all Kingdom citizens, walking in the truth of the Word of God. You are blessed and favored in the name of Jesus Christ, our Lord.

Shalom!

Contents

Introduction 11

1. The Key to Divine Intervention in Your Life.............................. 17
2. Your Source of Boldness 32
3. God's Mercy Is Extended to You 43
4. Because God Is Your Defense, You Are More Than
   a Conqueror 62
5. Why Do We Need a Defender?... 77
6. You Must Trust Fully Your Advocate and Protector................. 88
7. How Is All This Accomplished? 99
8. Dare to Be in Control of the Territory God Has Given You.. 116
9. Wake Up! Wisdom Is Your Key 130
10. How to Get Wisdom 141
11. Get Your Thinking Straight.. 148
12. Refuse to Be Stranded 164
13. Jesus Christ, the Name Above All Names................................ 178
14. The Great Shift... 194
15. Every Provision Is to Be Found in His Name 206

16. Wealth and Power Reside in His Name 220

17. Everything We Do must Be Done in the Name of Jesus 233

18. Ruled by the Spirit 243

Other Books by Dr. Abiola Idowu 257

Author Contact Information 263

The Spirit itself beareth witness with our spirit, that we are the children of God: and if children, then heirs; heirs of God, and JOINT-HEIRS WITH CHRIST.

—Romans 8:16-17

INTRODUCTION

The death, resurrection, and ascension of Jesus Christ brought in a new life and a new destiny in God that connected us to the same inheritance that Jesus Christ received from His heavenly Father. The Bible says clearly that we are heirs of God and joint heirs with Christ. But you cannot appreciate your new status until you know what Jesus Christ received and accept the fact that you are an heir together with Him. In this book, the Holy Spirit will open your eyes to your true status in God through Jesus Christ and how you can fully enjoy your inheritance in Him.

The Bible declares that the Father loves the Son and has *"given all things into His hand"*:

The Father loveth the Son, and hath given all things into his hand.

John 3:35

So, all things are in the hands of Jesus Christ, and that means all things are in your hands too, for you are a joint heir with Jesus. Based on this knowledge, it's time that you disallow the enemy from taking you for a ride. You must determine that never again will sickness and diseases, lack and oppression be your portion. Why? Because you are a joint heir with Christ. It is ignorance of the facts that makes a child of God live in fear and despair. You must rise to a new spiritual level because you have been chosen by the Almighty Himself:

According as he hath chosen us in him before the foundation of the world, that we should be holy and without blame before him in love. Ephesians 1:4

Christ is the ruler of everything, and He is, therefore, in charge of everything. The blessing of God upon us does not come from humans; it comes from Heaven. Therefore, we are not limited by earthly resources as others are. We have been chosen by God.

To be chosen is to be picked out from among the multitudes, to be separated for a particular purpose. You and I have been chosen by God to be holy and blameless. It doesn't matter what we may feel. We are blameless before Him because we have been freed from every evil entanglement.

Verse 7 of that chapter says that Father God purchased our freedom by the blood of Jesus Christ and, in this way, forgave our sins:

> *He is so rich in kindness and grace that he purchased our freedom with the blood of his Son and forgave our sins.*
> Ephesians 1:7, NLT

I have no sins; all my sins have been fully paid for. So, now, I cannot be judged, I cannot be punished, and I am blessed without measure in Christ. What could be more wonderful?

The most glorious aspect of this new life in Christ is that I also have access to all wisdom and understanding:

> *He has showered his kindness on us, along with all wisdom and understanding.*
> Ephesians 1:8, NLT

You can enjoy the ride for free through eternity because Jesus Christ already paid your fare and, because of that, everything is available for you now:

> *The Lord knoweth the thoughts of the wise, that they are vain. Therefore let no man glory in men. For all things are yours.*
> 1 Corinthians 3:20-21

The greatest news is that the life of God in us has given us a new status, the same status, in fact, that Jesus has, and God also has given us the same seat as He gave Jesus:

> *For he raised us from the dead along with Christ and seated us with him in the*

heavenly realms because we are united with Christ Jesus. So God can point to us in all future ages as examples of the incredible wealth of his grace and kindness toward us, as shown in all he has done for us who are united with Christ Jesus.

Ephesians 2:6-7, NLT

"I tell you the truth, anyone who believes in me will do the same works I have done, and even greater works, because I am going to be with the Father." John 14:12, NLT

"You don't have enough faith," Jesus told them. "I tell you the truth, if you had faith even as small as a mustard seed, you could say to this mountain, 'Move from here to there,' and it would move. Nothing would be impossible." Matthew 17:20, NLT

What does that mean? It means that whatever comes into your hands must multiply just as things did for Jesus. What the majority of people don't seem to understand is that a natural person cannot fulfill the mandate which God planned for mankind long ago. Adam "messed up" that chance, but in Christ Jesus, a new species of people is being created to fulfill that mandate, and these will do it supernaturally. They are not fallen men and women; they are a new creation in Christ Jesus:

> *For we are God's masterpiece. He has created us anew in Christ Jesus, so we can do the good things he planned for us long ago.* Ephesians 2:10, NLT

The Bible calls us a *"masterpiece."* There are other pieces, but we are the *"masterpiece."* As a *"masterpiece,"* we have been given the wonderful name of Jesus Christ to dominate the world around us and to create a territory for ourselves that is inaccessible to Satan and his forces of darkness. And it's all for the glory of our God.

Welcome to a new world of results, impact, and glory in the name of Jesus Christ. Yes, we are *Joint Heirs with Christ.*

Bishop Abiola Idowu
Jacksonville, Florida

CHAPTER 1

THE KEY TO DIVINE INTERVENTION IN YOUR LIFE

The LORD is merciful and compassionate,
slow to get angry and filled with
unfailing love.
The LORD is good to everyone.
He showers compassion on all his
creation.   Psalm 145:8-9, NLT

It is the nature of God that confers upon us His help. God is love. He does not *have* love; He *is* love. God is *"merciful and compassionate."* God's love could never see you drowning and not act to save your life. Jesus said:

> *Come unto me, all ye that labour and are heavy laden, and I will give you rest.*
>
> Matthew 11:28

Paul declared:

> *Now unto him that is able to do exceeding abundantly above all that we ask or think, according to the power that worketh in us,* Ephesians 3:20

We can experience in Christ the solution to all things, and therefore, as believers, we should no longer live without having tangible results:

> *Look unto me, and be ye saved, all the ends of the earth: for I am God, and there is none else.* Isaiah 45:22

> *So Christ was once offered to bear the sins of many; and unto them that look for him shall he appear the second time without sin unto salvation.*
>
> Hebrews 9:28

God is not just looking for our faults to bring to us judgement, as many believe. That is not His nature:

> *He will not always chide: neither will he keep his anger for ever. He hath not dealt with us after our sins; nor rewarded us according to our iniquities. For as the heaven is high above the earth, so great is his mercy toward them that fear him.* Psalm 103:9-11

Yes, God purges us, but He does it to make us the best we can be:

> *By mercy and truth iniquity is purged: and by the fear of the LORD men depart from evil.* Proverbs 16:6

But God will only do this if we allow Him to:

> *And Joshua said unto the people, Sanctify yourselves: for to morrow the LORD will do wonders among you.* Joshua 3:5

In other words, "Set yourself apart, and you will see the wonders of God." That was spoken under the old covenant, not the new. Under the new covenant, we are already set apart to experience wonders. In Christ, we are unstoppable, untouchable, and holy unto God:

But of him are ye in Christ Jesus, who of God is made unto us wisdom, and righteousness, and sanctification, and redemption: 1 Corinthians 1:30

And such were some of you: but ye are washed, but ye are sanctified, but ye are justified in the name of the Lord Jesus, and by the Spirit of our God.
1 Corinthians 6:11

Yet now he has reconciled you to himself through the death of Christ in his physical body. As a result, he has brought you into his own presence, and you are holy and blameless as you stand before him without a single fault.   Colossians 1:22, NLT

*So now we can rejoice in our wonderful
new relationship with God because our
Lord Jesus Christ has made us friends
of God.* Romans 5:11, NLT

*But those who fail to develop in this way
are shortsighted or blind, forgetting that
they have been cleansed from their old
sins.* 2 Peter 1:9, NLT

The legality of our status with God is the reason for us receiving divine help. We are now
children of the living God, and our resultant
benefits are based on sonship. That makes us
a living wonder to everyone around us.

But in order to be unstoppable, you must
know who you are and believe it with all
your heart. This truth is based on the following principles:

UNDERSTANDING YOUR TRUE IDENTITY

Since the garden of Eden, identity has
been a challenge for all mankind. Many

love God but never seem to come to know how God sees them. Adam "messed up" because of ignorance of his legality and true identity. God had said, "Don't eat the fruit of the tree of the knowledge of good and evil, and the day you eat it, you will surely die."

Then Satan came along and said, "Eat it, and you will be like God."

But Adam and Eve were like God already. Still, they allowed themselves to be swindled by the lies of the wicked one. Adam was already in charge, running the whole earth. He was created in the image and likeness of God, and yet he allowed someone to rob him of his great inheritance. How sad! Don't you make the same mistake.

But God never changed His mind concerning Adam. "Who told you that you were naked?" He asked.

Today, Satan is still using the same gimmicks and still operating in the same way. He is constantly trying to convince men and women that they are mere humans, but that is not our identity as believers in

Christ! Satan says, "You're very sick," "You can't make it," "People don't like you," "You'll never succeed at anything," etc. Far too many accept his lies and are sent out of their garden of influence.

Believe me, in Christ you are legally a child of the Almighty, and Christ is in you. You were born to be extraordinarily successful, and you carry the power of God in you right now. You are, therefore, unstoppable. Hallelujah! Do you believe it?

The Christ who is in Jesus is the same Christ who is in me and in you:

> *To whom God would make known what is the riches of the glory of this mystery among the Gentiles; which is Christ in you, the hope of glory.*
> Colossians 1:27

Now glory follows you everywhere you go. Jesus is not just our Savior; He is our Substitute. He represents us now in Heaven, and we represent Him here on earth.

UNDERSTANDING THAT YOUR LEGAL STATUS IS BASED ON GOD'S LOVE

You could never understand the depths of God's love for you and not be convinced that you are unstoppable and qualified for divine help:

> *For God so loved the world, that he gave his only begotten Son, that whosoever believeth in him should not perish, but have everlasting life.* John 3:16

That is your escape from the perils of life and death. Paul wrote:

> *Much more then, being now justified by his blood, we shall be saved from wrath through him. For if, when we were enemies, we were reconciled to God by the death of his Son, much more, being reconciled, we shall be saved by his life.* Romans 5:9-10

A good shepherd would lay down his life for his sheep. He would never allow a wolf to come in. Never! Jesus said:

I am the door: by me if any man enter in, he shall be saved, and shall go in and out, and find pasture. The thief cometh not, but for to steal, and to kill, and to destroy: I am come that they might have life, and that they might have it more abundantly. I am the good shepherd: the good shepherd giveth his life for the sheep. But he that is an hireling, and not the shepherd, whose own the sheep are not, seeth the wolf coming, and leaveth the sheep, and fleeth: and the wolf catcheth them, and scattereth the sheep. The hireling fleeth, because he is an hireling, and careth not for the sheep.

I am the good shepherd, and know my sheep, and am known of mine. As the Father knoweth me, even so know I the Father: and I lay down my life for the sheep. …

My Father, which gave them me, is greater than all; and no man is able to pluck them out of my Father's hand.

John 10:9-15 and 29

The legal status we gain because of God's love for us is the reason for our supreme confidence. The love of God is undeniably real, and there is nothing you can do to make Him love you more or to love you less. There are, however, things you can do to prove that you receive God's love. This is called faith in action. The action you take is the proof of your faith. If you believe that Father God loves you and that you are truly made in His image, then you will serve Him.

It is our individual responsibility to commit to all that God has promised. It is a choice, not a gift, nor a natural talent. It is a choice that all wise men and woman of faith make:

> *The LORD God hath opened mine ear, and I was not rebellious, neither turned away back.* Isaiah 50:5

God shows no favoritism for age or color. It is your decision to serve Him that makes you fruitful and energized. Jesus said:

Henceforth I call you not servants; for the servant knoweth not what his lord doeth: but I have called you friends; for all things that I have heard of my Father I have made known unto you. Ye have not chosen me, but I have chosen you, and ordained you, that ye should go and bring forth fruit, and that your fruit should remain: that whatsoever ye shall ask of the Father in my name, he may give it you. John 15:15-16

Serving God means bearing fruit for Him. Your service will be tested, and the result will reveal your decision. And you are not the only one who will know about it. In Daniel's time, King Nebuchadnezzar said to the three Hebrew men in the fiery furnace, *"Ye servants of the most high God, come forth"*:

Then Nebuchadnezzar came near to the mouth of the burning fiery furnace, and spake, and said, Shadrach, Meshach, and Abednego, ye servants of the most high God, come forth, and come hither.

Then Shadrach, Meshach, and Abednego, came forth of the midst of the fire. And the princes, governors, and captains, and the king's counsellors, being gathered together, saw these men, upon whose bodies the fire had no power, nor was an hair of their head singed, neither were their coats changed, nor the smell of fire had passed on them. Daniel 3:26-27

Everyone knew that these three men were servants of the living God. When we make serving God a way of life, others will see it:

Praise ye the LORD. Blessed is the man that feareth the LORD, that delighteth greatly in his commandments. His seed shall be mighty upon earth: the generation of the upright shall be blessed. Wealth and riches shall be in his house: and his righteousness endureth for ever. Psalm 112:1-3

Your complete yieldedness to God and His plan for your life is the key to achieving greatness. Paul wrote to the Roman believers:

> *Greet Mary, who bestowed much labour on us.* Romans 16:6

Your life of faithfulness and godly action will move the Father to see to your greatness:

> *By myself have I sworn, saith the LORD, for because thou hast done this thing, and hast not withheld thy son, thine only son: that in blessing I will bless thee, and in multiplying I will multiply thy seed as the stars of the heaven, and as the sand which is upon the sea shore; and thy seed shall possess the gate of his enemies; and in thy seed shall all the nations of the earth be blessed; because thou hast obeyed my voice.*
> Genesis 22:16-18

> *And I will bless them that bless thee, and curse him that curseth thee: and*

> *in thee shall all families of the earth be*
> *blessed.* Genesis 12:3

Stop begging God to lift you up. Get there by faithfully serving Him:

> *And ye shall serve the Lord your God,*
> *and he shall bless thy bread, and thy*
> *water; and I will take sickness away*
> *from the midst of thee.* Exodus 23:25

> *And he said unto him, Well, thou good*
> *servant: because thou hast been faithful*
> *in a very little, have thou authority over*
> *ten cities.* Luke 19:17

> *If any man serve me, let him follow me;*
> *and where I am, there shall also my ser-*
> *vant be: if any man serve me, him will*
> *my Father honour.* John 12:26

The help you seek from God is present with you now. Make up your mind to serve Him, and He will honor you.

Father, in the name of Jesus Christ, I receive help today in this area of my life. I am sanctified. Therefore, wonders are a must for my life.

Father, in the name of Jesus Christ, I receive grace to serve You unconditionally, grace to be a worthy ambassador, a soul winner. I take it now.

Yes, we are *Joint Heirs with Christ* and, because of it, the world will see that we are different.

CHAPTER 2

YOUR SOURCE OF BOLDNESS

Let us therefore come boldly unto the throne of grace, that we may obtain mercy, and find grace to help in time of need. Hebrews 4:16

God has said that you and I can come boldly to the throne of grace. That's access to Heaven itself. If we are to achieve greatness, we must have this source of boldness.

Goodness and mercy cannot be following you, and you are expecting calamity and destruction. Never! Let your faith be in the love of God for you, and every fear will disappear:

And we have known and believed the love that God hath to us. God is love; and he that dwelleth in love dwelleth in God, and God in him. 1 John 4:16

I know that no matter what is going on in my life, Father God will show up and intervene on my behalf:

When thou passest through the waters, I will be with thee; and through the rivers, they shall not overflow thee: when thou walkest through the fire, thou shalt not be burned; neither shall the flame kindle upon thee. Isaiah 43:2

Why is God so bent on protecting us? His response to us is based on several factors.

THE ADVOCACY OF OUR HIGH PRIEST, JESUS CHRIST

Winning a case in court depends a lot on your attorney. Even when most everyone thinks you should be jailed or prosecuted, a skilled attorney may turn the situation around through wise court proceedings. Well, your Judge is God, but Your Attorney is Jesus Christ Himself:

> *My little children, these things write I unto you, that ye sin not. And if any man sin, we have an advocate with the Father, Jesus Christ the righteous.*
>
> 1 John 2:1

> *Who shall lay any thing to the charge of God's elect? It is God that justifieth. Who is he that condemneth? It is Christ that died, yea rather, that is risen again, who is even at the right hand of God, who also maketh intercession for us.*
>
> Romans 8:33-34

You can't lose your case. God has made sure of that because of His love, compassion, and mercy. Again:

> *The LORD is gracious, and full of compassion; slow to anger, and of great*

34

mercy. The LORD is good to all: and his tender mercies are over all his works.

Psalm 145:8-9

Blessed be God, even the Father of our Lord Jesus Christ, the Father of mercies, and the God of all comfort.

2 Corinthians 1:3

But God, who is rich in mercy, for his great love wherewith he loved us, even when we were dead in sins, hath quickened us together with Christ, (by grace ye are saved;) and hath raised us up together, and made us sit together in heavenly places in Christ Jesus: that in the ages to come he might shew the exceeding riches of his grace in his kindness toward us through Christ Jesus.

Ephesians 2:4-7

The work of the High Priest in ancient times was to bring acceptable sacrifices before God to plead for His mercy for the people:

> *And Aaron took as Moses commanded, and ran into the midst of the congregation; and, behold, the plague was begun among the people: and he put on incense, and made an atonement for the people. And he stood between the dead and the living; and the plague was stayed.* Numbers 16:47-48

Jesus Christ, the beloved Son of God, is our great High Priest, and He intervenes on our behalf to stop every plague determined to destroy us:

> *But Christ being come an high priest of good things to come, by a greater and more perfect tabernacle, not made with hands, that is to say, not of this building; neither by the blood of goats and calves, but by his own blood he entered in once into the holy place, having obtained eternal redemption for us.*
> Hebrews 9:11-12

The widow of Nain experienced God's love through the arrival of Jesus:

And it came to pass the day after, that he [Jesus] went into a city called Nain; and many of his disciples went with him, and much people. Now when he came nigh to the gate of the city, behold, there was a dead man carried out, the only son of his mother, and she was a widow: and much people of the city was with her. And when the Lord saw her, he had compassion on her, and said unto her, Weep not. And he came and touched the bier: and they that bare him stood still. And he said, Young man, I say unto thee, Arise. And he that was dead sat up, and began to speak. And he delivered him to his mother. Luke 7:11-15

It's your turn now. Jesus stands before the Judge of the whole Universe to plead your case, and trust me, He always wins.

Standing at the tomb of Lazarus, His friend, Jesus prayed:

Father, I thank thee that thou hast heard me. And I knew that thou hearest me always: but because of the people which

> *stand by I said it, that they may believe*
> *that thou hast sent me.* John 11:41-42

Yes, Father God always heard Jesus, and He always hears you too. What qualifies you for access and wonders is God's intervention on your behalf.

YOUR BOLDNESS IS BASED ON YOUR AMBASSADORIAL POSITION

> *Now then we are ambassadors for*
> *Christ.*   2 Corinthians 5:20

We are God's representatives here on earth, and therefore, we are untouchable by the power of the enemy. You would never touch an ambassador of the United States to Russia. Never! In the same way, God said that he who touches you touches "the apple of His eye":

> *For thus saith the LORD of hosts; After*
> *the glory hath he sent me unto the*

nations which spoiled you: for he that toucheth you toucheth the apple of his eye. Zechariah 2:8

God has made us His friends and partners:

For we are labourers together with God: ye are God's husbandry, ye are God's building. According to the grace of God which is given unto me, as a wise masterbuilder, I have laid the foundation, and another buildeth thereon. But let every man take heed how he buildeth thereupon. For other foundation can no man lay than that is laid, which is Jesus Christ. 1 Corinthians 3:9-11

There are no weak, unimportant, poor, and devastated representative of Jesus Christ on earth. Some, however, fail to realize the authority they carry:

Then he called his twelve disciples together, and gave them power and authority over all devils, and to cure diseases. And he sent them to preach the kingdom of God, and to heal the sick. And he said unto them, Take nothing for your journey, neither staves, nor scrip, neither bread, neither money; neither have two coats apiece.   Luke 9:1-3

There is such favor and grace working on your behalf that wherever you go, you will be welcomed. The same honor that was upon Jesus as He walked the earth is now upon you:

He that heareth you heareth me; and he that despiseth you despiseth me; and he that despiseth me despiseth him that sent me.   Luke 10:16

If you believe what God has said, then activate it now. Become a soul-winner for your King and His Kingdom:

After these things the Lord appointed other seventy also, and sent them two and two before his face into every city and place, whither he himself would come. ...

And heal the sick that are therein, and say unto them, The kingdom of God is come nigh unto you. ...

And the seventy returned again with joy, saying, Lord, even the devils are subject unto us through thy name.

And he said unto them, I beheld Satan as lightning fall from heaven. Behold, I give unto you power to tread on serpents and scorpions, and over all the power of the enemy: and nothing shall by any means hurt you. Luke 10:1, 9 and 17-19

Declare God's Word and give your High Priest something to work with (your confession, the sacrifice, the fruit of your lips that the High Priest uses for your wholeness):

Seeing then that we have a great high priest, that is passed into the heavens, Jesus the Son of God, let us hold fast our profession. Hebrews 4:14

Father, based on Your Word, I declare that I am untouchable by any opposing force and power. I am blessed and exceptional in Jesus' name.

Father, because of what You have said, my heavens are opened now. I am favored, and I receive divine help now in Jesus' name.

Yes, we are *Joint Heirs with Christ* and, because of it, the world will see that we are different.

CHAPTER 3

GOD'S MERCY IS EXTENDED TO YOU

And they came to Jericho: and as he went out of Jericho with his disciples and a great number of people, blind Bartimaeus, the son of Timaeus, sat by the highway side begging. And when he heard that it was Jesus of Nazareth, he began to cry out, and say, Jesus, thou son of David, have mercy on me. And many charged him that he should hold his peace: but he cried the more a great deal, Thou son of David, have mercy on me. Mark 10:46-48

What did the blind man mean when he prayed for God's mercy to be extended to him? Mercy is God's desire to help the undeserving. His desire is to lift the downtrodden and the oppressed, to bring you and me to the top, especially when every door and gate seems to be closed to us.

The situation of blind Bartimaeus was severe. But remember that our God is the God of the whole Universe, and nothing is too hard for Him. His mercy can change anything and everything. He said so Himself:

> *Behold, I am the LORD , the God of all flesh: is there any thing too hard for me?* Jeremiah 32:27

Isaiah confirmed this sentiment:

> *For the LORD God will help me; therefore shall I not be confounded: therefore have I set my face like a flint, and I know that I shall not be ashamed. He is near that justifieth me; who will contend with me? let us stand together: who is mine*

adversary? let him come near to me. Behold, the LORD God will help me; who is he that shall condemn me? lo, they all shall wax old as a garment; the moth shall eat them up. Isaiah 50:7-9

The Kingdom of God is all about good news:

And it came to pass afterward, that he went throughout every city and village, preaching and shewing the glad tidings of the kingdom of God: and the twelve were with him. Luke 8:1

This good news is not just for our spirits; it also affects our physical reality. In response to the question of John the Baptist as to whether or not Jesus was the real Messiah, Jesus told His disciples to go and tell John, *"The blind see, the lame walk, the lepers are cleansed, the deaf hear, the dead are raised, to the poor the gospel is preached"*:

When the men were come unto him, they said, John Baptist hath sent us unto thee,

45

saying, Art thou he that should come? or look we for another? And in that same hour he cured many of their infirmities and plagues, and of evil spirits; and unto many that were blind he gave sight.

Then Jesus answering said unto them, Go your way, and tell John what things ye have seen and heard; how that the blind see, the lame walk, the lepers are cleansed, the deaf hear, the dead are raised, to the poor the gospel is preached. Luke 7:20-22

It's your turn today. Based on who God is and what He can do, be expectant. He is with you. Let this truth settle into your spirt. God has given us *"all things that pertain unto life and godliness through the knowledge of him":*

According as his divine power hath given unto us all things that pertain unto life and godliness, through the knowledge of him that hath called us to glory and virtue. 2 Peter 1:3

The value God has placed upon your life, as a child of God is the reason you can expect His intervention when you need it:

Are not five sparrows sold for two farthings, and not one of them is forgotten before God? But even the very hairs of your head are all numbered. Fear not therefore: ye are of more value than many sparrows. ...
Consider the ravens: for they neither sow nor reap; which neither have storehouse nor barn; and God feedeth them: how much more are ye better than the fowls?   Luke 12:6-7 and 24

It is the cost that determines the value of a thing, and believe me, you are costly. You are not ordinary at all. You are a wonder. It is a faith problem that brings us burdens. God has already given us all that we need for life:

If then God so clothe the grass, which is to day in the field, and to morrow is cast into

> *the oven; how much more will he clothe*
> *you, O ye of little faith?*   Luke 12:28

You are clothed, and there is no room for any shame in your life.

One of the ways God's mercy is extended to you is through angelic intervention. When angels come to your rescue, the help you need comes speedily, and nothing can prevent it.

You and I belong to a Kingdom that is organized and designed to take us to the Promised Land no matter what stands in our way. The angels of God go before us to clear the way. This is their assignment, to assist the saints of God:

> *Are they not all ministering spirits, sent*
> *forth to minister for them who shall be*
> *heirs of salvation?*   Hebrews 1:14

> *Behold, I send an Angel before thee, to*
> *keep thee in the way, and to bring thee*
> *into the place which I have prepared.*
>   Exodus 23:20

Angels are not human; they are heavenly beings that no man can box in:

> *Bless the* LORD *, ye his angels, that excel in strength, that do his commandments, hearkening unto the voice of his word.*
> Psalm 103:20

Where men lock a door, angels can still open it:

> *And they said, Stand back. And they said again, This one fellow came in to sojourn, and he will needs be a judge: now will we deal worse with thee, than with them. And they pressed sore upon the man, even Lot, and came near to break the door. But the men put forth their hand, and pulled Lot into the house to them, and shut to the door. And they smote the men that were at the door of the house with blindness, both small and great: so that they wearied themselves to find the door.* Genesis 19:9-11

The help that comes to you from angels makes it your turn to shine. When angels appeared at the tomb of Jesus, the obstacles, the keepers, the stumbling blocks, *"became as dead men"*:

> *And, behold, there was a great earth-quake: for the angel of the Lord descended from heaven, and came and rolled back the stone from the door, and sat upon it. His countenance was like lightning, and his raiment white as snow: and for fear of him the keepers did shake, and became as dead men.*
>
> Matthew 28:2-4

Whatever stands against your advancement is paralyzed now in Jesus' name.

Please get this truth: nobody on earth can stop the glory of the holy angels from shining, and therefore, you are designed for the top:

> *There shall no evil befall thee, neither shall any plague come nigh thy dwelling.*

For he shall give his angels charge over thee, to keep thee in all thy ways. They shall bear thee up in their hands, lest thou dash thy foot against a stone. Thou shalt tread upon the lion and adder: the young lion and the dragon shalt thou trample under feet. Psalm 91:10-13

Angelic help is available to you now. Angels are assigned to minister to you because you are saved. Even when we go to church, we are in the midst of *"an innumerable company of angels"*:

But ye are come unto mount Sion, and unto the city of the living God, the heavenly Jerusalem, and to an innumerable company of angels, to the general assembly and church of the firstborn, which are written in heaven, and to God the Judge of all, and to the spirits of just men made perfect, and to Jesus the mediator of the new covenant, and to the blood of sprinkling, that speaketh better things than that of Abel. Hebrews 12:22-24

That's why the enemy gives you so many excuses not to attend God's house. He wants to deny you your blessings. He sees the potential you carry and know angels are present to help you maximize that potential:

> *But we have this treasure in earthen vessels, that the excellency of the power may be of God, and not of us.*
>
> 2 Corinthians 4:7

In Moses' day, angels formed a pillar of cloud by day and a pillar of fire by night, so that the people were securely protected on their way to the Promised Land. You can set goals, and angles will help you achieve them:

> *And the angel of God, which went before the camp of Israel, removed and went behind them; and the pillar of the cloud went from before their face, and stood behind them.* Exodus 14:19

> *For mine Angel shall go before thee, and bring thee in unto the Amorites,*

*and the Hittites, and the Perizzites, and
the Canaanites, the Hivites, and the
Jebusites: and I will cut them off.*
Exodus 23:23

Just knowing that angels exist will not
cause them to work on your behalf. You
must release them into action through your
prayers and declarations based on God's
Word:

*And when he had apprehended him, he
put him in prison, and delivered him to
four quaternions of soldiers to keep him;
intending after Easter to bring him forth
to the people. Peter therefore was kept
in prison: but prayer was made without
ceasing of the church unto God for him.
And when Herod would have brought
him forth, the same night Peter was
sleeping between two soldiers, bound
with two chains: and the keepers before
the door kept the prison. And, behold,
the angel of the Lord came upon him,
and a light shined in the prison: and he*

> *smote Peter on the side, and raised him up, saying, Arise up quickly. And his chains fell off from his hands.*
>
> Acts 12:4-7

When Jesus was praying and fasting in the wilderness, angels came and ministered to Him. Pray and you, too, will experience angelic interventions.

An amazing thing happened to Daniel:

> *In the third year of Cyrus king of Persia a thing was revealed unto Daniel, whose name was called Belteshazzar; and the thing was true, but the time appointed was long: and he understood the thing, and had understanding of the vision*
> *In those days I Daniel was mourning three full weeks. I ate no pleasant bread, neither came flesh nor wine in my mouth, neither did I anoint myself at all, till three whole weeks were fulfilled. And in the four and twentieth day of the first month, as I was by the side of the great river, which is Hiddekel; then*

I lifted up mine eyes, and looked, and behold a certain man clothed in linen, whose loins were girded with fine gold of Uphaz: his body also was like the beryl, and his face as the appearance of lightning, and his eyes as lamps of fire, and his arms and his feet like in colour to polished brass, and the voice of his words like the voice of a multitude.

And I Daniel alone saw the vision: for the men that were with me saw not the vision; but a great quaking fell upon them, so that they fled to hide themselves. Therefore I was left alone, and saw this great vision, and there remained no strength in me: for my comeliness was turned in me into corruption, and I retained no strength. Yet heard I the voice of his words: and when I heard the voice of his words, then was I in a deep sleep on my face, and my face toward the ground.

And, behold, an hand touched me, which set me upon my knees and upon the palms of my hands. And he said unto me, O Daniel, a man greatly beloved, understand the words that I speak unto thee, and stand upright: for unto thee am I now sent. And when he had spoken this word unto me, I stood trembling.

Then said he unto me, Fear not, Daniel: for from the first day that thou didst set thine heart to understand, and to chasten thyself before thy God, thy words were heard, and I am come for thy words. But the prince of the kingdom of Persia withstood me one and twenty days: but, lo, Michael, one of the chief princes, came to help me; and I remained there with the kings of Persia. Now I am come to make thee understand what shall befall thy people in the latter days: for yet the vision is for many days. And when he had spoken such words unto me, I set my face toward the ground, and I became dumb. And, behold, one like the similitude of the sons of men touched my lips: then I opened my mouth, and spake, and said unto him that stood before me,

O my lord, by the vision my sorrows are turned upon me, and I have retained no strength. For how can the servant of this my lord talk with this my lord? for as for me, straightway there remained no strength in me, neither is there breath left in me.

Then there came again and touched me one like the appearance of a man, and he strengthened me, and said, O man greatly beloved, fear not: peace be unto thee, be strong, yea, be strong. And when he had spoken unto me, I was strengthened, and said, Let my lord speak; for thou hast strengthened me.

Then said he, Knowest thou wherefore I come unto thee? and now will I return to fight with the prince of Persia: and when I am gone forth, lo, the prince of Grecia shall come. But I will shew thee that which is noted in the scripture of truth: and there is none that holdeth with me in these things, but Michael your prince. Daniel 10:1-21

Angels respond when you speak God's Word. Again:

> *Bless the* LORD, *ye his angels, that excel in strength, that do his commandments, hearkening unto the voice of his word.*
> Psalm 103:20

Anything is possible when you declare the truth of the Scriptures.

The moment Mary agreed with the Word spoken to her, she became pregnant. Her answer to the angel was:

> *Behold the handmaid of the Lord; be it unto me according to thy word. And the angel departed from her.*   Luke 1:38

The wise King Solomon wrote:

> *Suffer not thy mouth to cause thy flesh to sin; neither say thou before the angel, that it was an error: wherefore should God be angry at thy voice, and destroy the work of thine hands?*   Ecclesiastes 5:6

Angels assigned to you are listening to what you say. They take your word to be your will, and you can cause them to move into action when you speak God's words.

Jesus said:

> *For verily I say unto you, That whoso-*
> *ever shall say unto this mountain, Be*
> *thou removed, and be thou cast into the*
> *sea; and shall not doubt in his heart, but*
> *shall believe that those things which he*
> *saith shall come to pass; he shall have*
> *whatsoever he saith.* Mark 11:23

When you acknowledge Jesus Christ and serve Him, and you speak Kingdom language, then angels are set to work on your behalf:

> *Then the high priest rose up, and all*
> *they that were with him, (which is the*
> *sect of the Sadducees,) and were filled*
> *with indignation, and laid their hands*
> *on the apostles, and put them in the*
> *common prison. But the angel of the*

Lord by night opened the prison doors, and brought them forth, and said, Go, stand and speak in the temple to the people all the words of this life.

But when the officers came, and found them not in the prison, they returned and told, saying, The prison truly found we shut with all safety, and the keepers standing without before the doors: but when we had opened, we found no man within.   Acts 5:17-20, and 22-23

This was exactly what Daniel experienced. An angel of God shut the mouths of the lions, so that he was not harmed. And God is no respecter of persons. Angels bring us good news and give us victories to the honor of Jesus Christ, but we must engage them:

And he went up from thence unto Bethel: and as he was going up by the way, there came forth little children out of the city, and mocked him, and said unto him, Go up, thou bald head; go up, thou bald head. And he turned back, and looked on them,

60

and cursed them in the name of the LORD. *And there came forth two she bears out of the wood, and tare forty and two children of them.* 2 Kings 2:23-24

Father, in the name of Jesus Christ, everything that has been set to hinder my destiny is cursed now.

God judgeth the righteous, and God is angry with the wicked every day. If he turn not, he will whet his sword; he hath bent his bow, and made it ready. He hath also prepared for him the instruments of death; he ordaineth his arrows against the persecutors. Psalm 7:11-13

Father, in the name of Jesus Christ, let whatever or whoever is intent upon hindering me come to a speedy demise for Your glory.

Yes, we are *Joint Heirs with Christ* and, because of it, the world will see that we are different.

CHAPTER 4

Because God Is Your Defense, You Are More Than a Conqueror

For the hurt of the daughter of my people am I hurt; I am black; astonishment hath taken hold on me. Is there no balm in Gilead; is there no physician there? why then is not the health of the daughter of my people recovered?

Jeremiah 8:21-22

Since the fall of man, man has been the target of the enemy, and his intention is to frustrate God Himself. He knows how much God loves men and women, boys and girls and will do everything within his power to cause men to doubt God's faithfulness. He attacks men and women so that God can feel their suffering. The only way he can hurt God is to hurt God's people.

But, as we have seen, God said that touching you is touching the apple of His eye.

For thus saith the LORD of hosts; After the glory hath he sent me unto the nations which spoiled you: for he that toucheth you toucheth the apple of his eye. Zechariah 2:8

God loves you and has vowed to defend you and bring you to a pleasurable life. Let Him do His work.

No matter what you do, some people will not like you. Leave their case in the hands of God, for He is your Defender.

There will be people sent by God into your life to cause you to be promoted. Some, like Judas Iscariot, the disciple of Jesus, will think they are doing you evil, but God will use what they do to turn your story around. So, when it seems that men are hurting you, don't get upset, and don't attempt to take revenge. When you do this, you push God away.

The people who stand against you cannot control your destiny:

> *Therefore thus saith the* LORD*; Behold, I will plead thy cause, and take vengeance for thee; and I will dry up her sea, and make her springs dry.*
>
> Jeremiah 51:36

Men were talking against Moses, but God heard them and punished them. When you are hated is often the time you will excel. So, don't be afraid to be controversial and take a stand for truth. God has your back.

Jesus taught:

> *And he said unto them, When ye pray, say, Our Father which art in heaven, Hallowed be thy name. Thy kingdom come. Thy will be done, as in heaven, so in earth.*
>
> Luke 11:2

God wants Heaven's experience to be repeated in your life here on earth. The unwavering faithfulness of God and the power of His covenant is your guarantee of divine protection:

> *God forbid: yea, let God be true, but every man a liar; as it is written, That thou mightest be justified in thy sayings, and mightest overcome when thou art judged.* Romans 3:4

God spoke to Abraham very clearly in this regard:

> *After these things the word of the LORD came unto Abram in a vision, saying, Fear not, Abram: I am thy shield, and thy exceeding great reward.*
> Genesis 15:1

This covenant word for Abraham stopped all the fiery anger of Abimalech, Pharaoh, the Philistines, and all others who raged against him and his generations. And, since we are children of Abraham, you and I are included in this promise through the grace of our Lord Jesus Christ:

> *And if ye be Christ's, then are ye Abraham's seed, and heirs according to the promise.* Galatians 3:29

It takes this understanding to successfully face the issues life will present. God is my defense! PERIOD!

David said to the giant who loomed over him, "You came to me with a sword and a spear, but I come against you *'in the name of the LORD of Hosts'*":

> *And David said to Saul, Let no man's heart fail because of him; thy servant will go and fight with this Philistine. ...*
> *Then said David to the Philistine, Thou comest to me with a sword, and with a spear, and with a shield: but I come to thee in the name of the LORD of hosts, the God of the armies of Israel, whom thou hast defied. This day will the LORD*

deliver thee into mine hand; and I will smite thee, and take thine head from thee; and I will give the carcases of the host of the Philistines this day unto the fowls of the air, and to the wild beasts of the earth; that all the earth may know that there is a God in Israel. And all this assembly shall know that the LORD saveth not with sword and spear: for the battle is the LORD's, and he will give you into our hands. 1 Samuel 17:32 and 45-47

The Bible, God's sacred and infallible Word, says:

The sun shall not smite thee by day, nor the moon by night.   Psalm 121:6

God has a plan to rescue you. His commitment to our safety, peace, and prosperity means we have a glorious destiny in Christ. God Himself is our Defense and our Shield. He has said that we are precious to Him and He will do whatever it takes to preserve and enhance our lives:

67

> *Since thou wast precious in my sight,*
> *thou hast been honourable, and I have*
> *loved thee: therefore will I give men for*
> *thee, and people for thy life.*
>
> Isaiah 43:4

> *No weapon that is formed against thee*
> *shall prosper; and every tongue that*
> *shall rise against thee in judgment thou*
> *shalt condemn. This is the heritage*
> *of the servants of the LORD, and their*
> *righteousness is of me, saith the LORD.*
>
> Isaiah 54:17

"No weapon that is formed against you shall prosper ... . This is the heritage of the servants of God." It does not matter how things might look; you cannot sink. Never! God is your defense.

The way Paul was rescued from the plots of the Jews of his day could only be because God was his defense:

> *And when there arose a great dissen-*
> *sion, the chief captain, fearing lest Paul*

should have been pulled in pieces of them, commanded the soldiers to go down, and to take him by force from among them, and to bring him into the castle.

And the night following the Lord stood by him, and said, Be of good cheer, Paul: for as thou hast testified of me in Jerusalem, so must thou bear witness also at Rome. Acts 23:10-11

And when it was day, certain of the Jews banded together, and bound themselves under a curse, saying that they would neither eat nor drink till they had killed Paul. And they were more than forty which had made this conspiracy. And they came to the chief priests and elders, and said, We have bound ourselves under a great curse, that we will eat nothing until we have slain Paul. Now therefore ye with the council signify to the chief captain that he bring him down unto you to morrow, as though ye would enquire something more perfectly concerning him: and we, or ever he come near, are ready to kill him.

And when Paul's sister's son heard of their lying in wait, he went and entered into the castle, and told Paul.

Then Paul called one of the centurions unto him, and said, Bring this young man unto the chief captain: for he hath a certain thing to tell him.

So he took him, and brought him to the chief captain, and said, Paul the prisoner called me unto him, and prayed me to bring this young man unto thee, who hath something to say unto thee.

Then the chief captain took him by the hand, and went with him aside privately, and asked him, What is that thou hast to tell me?

And he said, The Jews have agreed to desire thee that thou wouldest bring down Paul to morrow into the council, as though they would enquire somewhat of him more perfectly. But do not thou yield unto them: for there lie in wait for him of them more than forty men, which have bound themselves with an oath, that they will neither eat nor drink till they have killed him: and now are they ready, looking for a promise from thee. So the chief captain then let the young man depart, and charged him, See thou tell no man that thou hast shewed these things to me.

And he called unto him two centurions, saying, Make ready two hundred soldiers to go to Caesarea, and horsemen threescore and ten, and spearmen two hundred, at the third hour of the night; and provide them beasts, that they may set Paul on, and bring him safe unto Felix the governor. Acts 23:12-24

These people had vowed with a fast that Paul must be put to death, but God intervened, and no evil befell him. In the very same way, God has made provision to rescue you from the plans of the enemy and bring you out of every trial victorious. The great I AM is with you always.

When men were seeking Jesus the night of His arrest, He asked them, *"Who is it you want?"* When they answered, *"Jesus of Nazareth,"* and He said, *"I am he,"* they all fell to the ground:

> *So Judas came to the garden, guiding a detachment of soldiers and some officials from the chief priests and the Pharisees. They were carrying torches, lanterns and weapons. Jesus, knowing all that was going to happen to him, went out and asked them, "Who is it you want?"*
> *"Jesus of Nazareth," they replied.*
> *"I am he," Jesus said. (And Judas the traitor was standing there with them.) When Jesus said, "I am he," they drew back and fell to the ground.*
>
> John 18:3-6, NIV

This was not a small band of people. It was an entire *"detachment of soldiers,"* along with officials sent by the Chief Priests and the Pharisees, probably temple police. Some think there might have been as many as six hundred of them in all. Yet, when Jesus said, *"I am he,"* they all fell helplessly to the ground. Also affected was a young man who stood by:

> *A young man, wearing nothing but a linen garment, was following Jesus. When they seized him, he fled naked, leaving his garment behind.*
>
> Mark 14:51-52, NIV

Jesus Christ, without the need to call for reinforcements, overcame six hundred soldiers and policemen. He later said He could have called for legions of angels to come to His rescue:

> *Thinkest thou that I cannot now pray to my Father, and he shall presently give me more than twelve legions of angels?*
>
> Matthew 26:52

Angels are powerful! In fact, Isaiah 37:36 records that a single angel obliterated 185,000 men in one night. So, if a single angel had that kind of power, how much combined strength would there be in twelve legions of angels?

According to Rick Renner in his book, *Paid in Full*,[1] the fact that a single angel was able to obliterate 185,000 men in one night means the combined strength in a legion, about six thousand angels, would have been enough to destroy 1,110,000,000 men (that is 1 billion, 110 million), and that's just the combined power in one legion of angels!

If we multiply this number (185,000) by 12 legions, or at least 72,000 angels (this was the number of angels Jesus said were available to Him on the night of His arrest), we find that there was enough combined strength at Jesus' disposal to have annihilated at least 13,320,000,000 men (that is, 13 billion, 320 million men), more than twice the number of people living on the earth right now!

When Jesus said, "I am with you always," He meant it, and His presence is for our defence. In fact, one of the covenant names of God is Defense. That name is Jehovah-Nissi,

---

1. Self-Published in 2013

74

meaning Jehovah, Our Banner (see Exodus 17:15).

Become conscious of God's presence with you always. Knowing that He is not a man, that He can never lie, and that whatever He says becomes your strength can sustain you in hard times:

> *He that dwelleth in the secret place of the most High shall abide under the shadow of the Almighty. I will say of the* Lord, *He is my refuge and my fortress: my God; in him will I trust.* Psalm 91:1-2

God has provided this shield. Walk in this consciousness. Rest under His wings, and be conscious of the fact that He is protecting you. As the eagle cover its eaglets with its wings of protection, so the Lord covers you. Nothing can remove you from His protection as long as you make a conscious decision to dwell there:

> *My Father, which gave them me, is greater than all; and no man is able to pluck them out of my Father's hand.*   John 10:29

Keep me as the apple of the eye, hide me under the shadow of thy wings.

Psalm 17:8

He shall cover thee with his feathers, and under his wings shalt thou trust: his truth shall be thy shield and buckler.

Psalm 91:4

Don't say what God has not said:

I will say of the LORD, He is my refuge and my fortress: my God; in him will I trust. Surely he shall deliver thee from the snare of the fowler, and from the noisome pestilence. He shall cover thee with his feathers, and under his wings shalt thou trust: his truth shall be thy shield and buckler. Thou shalt not be afraid for the terror by night; nor for the arrow that flieth by day.

Psalm 91:2-5

Yes, we are *Joint Heirs with Christ* and, because of it, the world will see that we are different.

CHAPTER 5

WHY DO WE NEED A DEFENDER?

Yea, the Almighty shall be thy defence,
and thou shalt have plenty of silver.

Job 22:25

Why do we even need a defender? Because life is not a fun fair; it's warfare. There are giants to be faced, evil forces to be dealt with, and people who have vowed to bring us down at all cost. But relax, you are covered and protected. The Word of God says that even if they join hands against us, *"the wicked will not go unpunished: but the seed of the righteous shall be delivered"*:

Though hand join in hand, the wicked shall not be unpunished: but the seed of the righteous shall be delivered. Proverbs 11:21

Since God is for you, no man can prevail against you:

What shall we then say to these things? If God be for us, who can be against us? Romans 8:31

Jesus said:

But whoso shall offend one of these little ones which believe in me, it were better for him that a millstone were hanged about his neck, and that he were drowned in the depth of the sea. Woe unto the world because of offences! for it must needs be that offences come; but woe to that man by whom the offence cometh! Matthew 18:6-7

Whatever stands as an obstacle to your destiny is cursed today, for God is your defense:

When thou goest out to battle against thine enemies, and seest horses, and chariots, and a people more than thou, be not afraid of them: for the LORD thy God is with thee, which brought thee up out of the land of Egypt. And it shall be, when ye are come nigh unto the battle, that the priest shall approach and speak unto the people, and shall say unto them, Hear, O Israel, ye approach this day unto battle against your enemies: let not your hearts faint, fear not, and do not tremble, neither be ye terrified because of them; for the LORD your God is he that goeth with you, to fight for you against your enemies, to save you.

Deuteronomy 20:1-4

You can live a life free of worry and anxiety if you know your Father runs this entire Universe, and you are part of a great and victorious team:

For we are labourers together with God: ye are God's husbandry, ye are God's building. 1 Corinthians 3:9

79

Again, it is your position as His child that determines your status. Where God has placed you is the reason for your safety. The God of vengeance has vowed that no evil will touch you again forever in the name of Jesus Christ:

> *They shall not hurt nor destroy in all my holy mountain: for the earth shall be full of the knowledge of the* Lord, *as the waters cover the sea.*   Isaiah 11:9

God said He would be an enemy to your enemies and an adversary to your adversaries:

> *But if thou shalt indeed obey his voice, and do all that I speak; then I will be an enemy unto thine enemies, and an adversary unto thine adversaries.*   Exodus 23:22

The biblical declaration is:

> *Let God arise, let his enemies be scattered: let them also that hate him flee before him.*   Psalm 68:1

80

Your enemies will also be scattered. Welcome to God's wonderful world of peace and tranquility. Just as everything that Haman planned for Mordecai boomeranged, whatever is set against you will also boomerang. Whatever men say about you that is not true, stop defending yourself. Relax! The God of vengeance will take over your defense now.

David sang:

> *O God of vengeance, let your glorious justice shine forth!* Psalm 94:1, NLT

You need to sing that same song. The character of God forbids Him to allow anyone to oppress His children. He simply cannot allow it. He is a jealous God:

> *Thou shalt not bow down thyself to them, nor serve them: for I the LORD thy God am a jealous God, visiting the iniquity of the fathers upon the children unto the third and fourth generation of them that hate me.* Exodus 20:5

81

God doesn't want anyone touching His Bride.

Why is God fighting my battle, and what is the guarantee of my victory? Again, it is that I am an ambassador for Christ:

> *Now then we are ambassadors for Christ, as though God did beseech you by us: we pray you in Christ's stead, be ye reconciled to God.*
> 2 Corinthians 5:20

As an ambassador of Christ, you have immunity extended by the government of God to the earth. It's part of your employment package. You may not look qualified, but because you are God's candidate, He qualifies you. That makes you untouchable by any force on the earth. Why? Because you represent Heaven here below:

> *But we are citizens of heaven, where the Lord Jesus Christ lives. And we are eagerly waiting for him to return as our Savior.* Philippians 3:20, NLT

You are citizen of another country, a representative of your King, and because of it, there is a protection over you that you can hardly imagine. Paul was even protected from a poisonous snake:

> *Once we were safe on shore, we learned that we were on the island of Malta. The people of the island were very kind to us. It was cold and rainy, so they built a fire on the shore to welcome us.*
>
> *As Paul gathered an armful of sticks and was laying them on the fire, a poisonous snake, driven out by the heat, bit him on the hand. The people of the island saw it hanging from his hand and said to each other, "A murderer, no doubt! Though he escaped the sea, justice will not permit him to live." But Paul shook off the snake into the fire and was unharmed.*
>
> Acts 28:1-5, NLT

Because many believers do very little for their King, they feel unqualified to claim this protection. Even when he was approaching death, Hezekiah stood against it:

About that time Hezekiah became deathly ill, and the prophet Isaiah son of Amoz went to visit him. He gave the king this message: "This is what the LORD says: Set your affairs in order, for you are going to die. You will not recover from this illness."

When Hezekiah heard this, he turned his face to the wall and prayed to the LORD, "Remember, O LORD, how I have always been faithful to you and have served you single-mindedly, always doing what pleases you." Then he broke down and wept bitterly.

But before Isaiah had left the middle courtyard, this message came to him from the LORD: "Go back to Hezekiah, the leader of my people. Tell him, 'This is what the LORD, the God of your ancestor David, says: I have heard your prayer and seen your tears. I will heal you, and three days from now you will get out of bed and go to the Temple of the LORD. I will add fifteen years to your life, and I will rescue you and this city from the king of Assyria. I will defend this city for my own honor and for the sake of my servant David.'"

Then Isaiah said, "Make an ointment from figs." So Hezekiah's servants spread the ointment over the boil, and Hezekiah recovered! 2 Kings 20:1-7

Just as Hezekiah recovered and went on to live many more years, you can overcome too. How? Always remember that you have the whole armor of God at your disposal, so there is provision for your defense. God's instructions for their use are very clear, and so there is no reason to be afraid. The forces of darkness are real, but if you put on the whole armor of God, you will prevail.

Caution: your own armor will fail. Thank God for your armor. It may be education, money, or connections, but these cannot help you withstand in the evil day.

Here's what Paul wrote:

> *Finally, my brethren, be strong in the Lord, and in the power of his might. Put on the whole armour of God, that ye may be able to stand against the wiles of the devil. For we wrestle not against flesh and blood, but against principalities, against powers, against the rulers of the darkness of this world, against spiritual wickedness in high places.* Ephesians 6:10-12

You can stop the enemy at the gate with the armor God provides, but this armor must be put on by a conscious decision of faith. These elements are not physical, but they are no less real.

This was the armor David used when he faced Goliath and the same armor that protected Shadrach, Meshach, and Abednego from the fire, so that it could not burn them. It's your turn now. Put on the Christ and His truth, His righteousness, and prayer. Also put on the armor of humility, the armor of service, the armor of faith, and the armor of salvation.

Yes, we are *Joint Heirs with Christ* and, because of it, the world will see that we are different.

CHAPTER 6

YOU MUST TRUST FULLY YOUR ADVOCATE AND PROTECTOR

My little children, these things write I unto you, that ye sin not. And if any man sin, we have an advocate with the Father, Jesus Christ the righteous.

1 John 2:1

Jesus always pleads on your behalf, and His plea is "Not guilty!" Paul wrote:

There is therefore now no condemnation to them which are in Christ Jesus, who walk not after the flesh, but after the Spirit. Romans 8:1

Your Advocate presents enough evidence before the Judge to acquit you. This also means that you can escape sickness and disease through the stripes He bore for you. There is now no room for depression or even lack in the life of a believer. Jesus Christ was made poor so that you might be made rich, and it has all been fully paid:

> *For ye know the grace of our Lord Jesus Christ, that, though he was rich, yet for your sakes he became poor, that ye through his poverty might be rich.*
>
> 2 Corinthians 8:9

When you face the Judge, you can do so boldly because your Divine Attorney is at your side, and He has never lost a case.

Will God ever change? Never! He is a covenant-keeping God, an ever-faithful God, a never-failing God. He has exhibited a pattern of operations that prove His commitment to the defense of His people. He is always there to defend you—always!

God was in the ark with Noah and his family, and only they survived the great flood (see Genesis 6-9). He was with Abraham and his servants when they destroyed five enemy cities (see Genesis 14:8-15). He was with Elisha when the Syrian soldiers who threatened him were blinded (see 2 Kings 6). He is the same God whose presence was with Daniel, so that the lions could not hurt him (see Daniel 6). This God has made a covenant with you through our Lord Jesus Christ:

> *Ye are the children of the prophets, and of the covenant which God made with our fathers, saying unto Abraham, And in thy seed shall all the kindreds of the earth be blessed.* Acts 3:25

God has determined that not a hair of your head will fall without His approval:

> *But the very hairs of your head are all numbered.* Matthew 10:30

Because of the vigilance of our heavenly Father, nothing can come against us without His notice, and He knows how to cut off the best-laid plans of the enemy.

He is the King who saw a man without a wedding garment. Nobody seemed to know how the man got into the wedding feast, but the King knew how to get him out:

> *And when the king came in to see the guests, he saw there a man which had not on a wedding garment: and he saith unto him, Friend, how camest thou in hither not having a wedding garment? And he was speechless.*
>
> *Then said the king to the servants, Bind him hand and foot, and take him away, and cast him into outer darkness, there shall be weeping and gnashing of teeth. For many are called, but few are chosen.*
>
> Matthew 22:11-14

Whatever has entered into your life that is not pleasing to God must go today.

Understanding The Mystery of Jesus' Suffering

Understanding the mystery of Jesus' suffering gives you access to divine health and vitality. His substitutional sacrifice exempts you and me from every harassment of Satan and all his works:

> *He that committeth sin is of the devil;*
> *for the devil sinneth from the beginning.*
> *For this purpose the Son of God was*
> *manifested, that he might destroy the*
> *works of the devil.* 1 John 3:8

Allow what Jesus has already done on your behalf to manifest in your life today. Why should you suffer these attacks of the evil one? You are God's beloved child.

The Savior came to save us, and one of the major reasons He came was to give us wholeness in our bodies. He is *"the saviour of the body"*:

> *For the husband is the head of the*
> *wife, even as Christ is the head of the*

*church: and he is the saviour of the
body.*   Ephesians 5:23

Another of the covenant names of God
is Jehovah-Rapha. It means the Lord our
Healer, and therefore sickness and diseases
must not have dominion over those of us
who believe in Jesus. God promised:

> *If thou wilt diligently hearken to the
> voice of the LORD thy God, and wilt do
> that which is right in his sight, and wilt
> give ear to his commandments, and keep
> all his statutes, I will put none of these
> diseases upon thee, which I have brought
> upon the Egyptians: for I am the LORD
> that healeth thee.*   Exodus 15:26

Sickness and disease are distractions. They
demand our attention and take our focus off
of God. But God merits your full attention,
and sickness must not be allowed to hinder.
Sickness and disease are from the devil. He
may use circumstances to cause them, but
he is the author of them all.

We are being told by so-called "medical experts" that sickness is hereditary, but God is now your Father, and you certainly didn't get any sickness from Him. When man was sent out of the garden, he was exposed to his enemy, the devil, and the devil's mission, Jesus said, has always been *"to steal, and to kill, and to destroy"*:

> *The thief cometh not, but for to steal, and to kill, and to destroy: I am come that they might have life, and that they might have it more abundantly.*
>
> John 10:10

Jesus saw a woman in a pitiful physical condition. See what He thought had caused it:

> *And, behold, there was a woman which had a spirit of infirmity eighteen years, and was bowed together, and could in no wise lift up herself. And when Jesus saw her, he called her to him, and said unto her, Woman, thou art loosed from thine infirmity. ...*

And ought not this woman, being a daughter of Abraham, whom Satan hath bound, lo, these eighteen years, be loosed from this bond on the sabbath day?
Luke 13:11-12, and 16

According to Jesus, it was Satan who had bowed this woman down for so long, and He commanded her to be loosed. Yes, Satan does terrible things to people, but the good news is that Satan has been conquered by Christ Jesus. The stripes He took on the cross stripped Satan of all power over those who believe. Now Satan is nothing more than a toothless bulldog:

Forasmuch then as the children are partakers of flesh and blood, he also himself likewise took part of the same; that through death he might destroy him that had the power of death, that is, the devil. Hebrews 2:14

Jesus became our Substitute, and we were in Him when He conquered the devil. In the eyes of faith, we are the ones who conquered. God's provision for the cure was sending Jesus, His beloved Son, to set the captives free. Jesus said:

> *The people which sat in darkness saw great light; and to them which sat in the region and shadow of death light is sprung up.* Matthew 4:16

"The people which sat in darkness saw great light." Jesus is that Light. He told a blind man He met, *"As long as I am in the world, I am the light of the world":*

> *And as Jesus passed by, he saw a man which was blind from his birth. And his disciples asked him, saying, Master, who did sin, this man, or his parents, that he was born blind?*
> *Jesus answered, Neither hath this man sinned, nor his parents: but that the works of God should be made manifest in him. I must work the works of him that sent me, while it is day: the night*

cometh, when no man can work. As long as I am in the world, I am the light of the world. John 9:1-5

Where light reigns darkness has no place, and sickness is part of darkness. If you believe the promises of God and have become His child, you can no longer be ruled by the forces of the enemy. You can no longer be trapped in sickness and disease. You are no longer children of this world. You have left the world of darkness and been translated into the Kingdom of light:

> *Giving thanks unto the Father, which hath made us meet to be partakers of the inheritance of the saints in light: who hath delivered us from the power of darkness, and hath translated us into the kingdom of his dear Son: in whom we have redemption through his blood, even the forgiveness of sins.* Colossians 1:12-14

If that seems odd to you, then you need to become a child again and let God shift your thinking so that you can walk in the freedom He purchased. The world must know that God loves you just as He loves Jesus, and the demonstration of that love will be visible to all. Jesus said:

> *And the glory which thou gavest me I have given them; that they may be one, even as we are one.* John 17:22

Yes, we are *Joint Heirs with Christ* and, because of it, the world will see that we are different.

CHAPTER 7

HOW IS ALL THIS ACCOMPLISHED?

If the foundations be destroyed, what can the righteous do? Psalm 11:3

The integrity of the Word of God is the foundation for our confidence and faith. His Word heals and strengthens us, because God is in His Word:

He sent his word, and healed them, and delivered them from their destructions.
Psalm 107:20

Just as a man cannot save himself from sin, he also cannot heal himself of sickness and disease. But God laid our sickness and disease upon Jesus Christ, just as He laid our sins and iniquities upon Him, and He became our sacrifice for our total escape from darkness:

> *Yet it pleased the* LORD *to bruise him; he hath put him to grief: when thou shalt make his soul an offering for sin, he shall see his seed, he shall prolong his days, and the pleasure of the* LORD *shall prosper in his hand.*   Isaiah 53:10

> *The next day John seeth Jesus coming unto him, and saith, Behold the Lamb of God, which taketh away the sin of the world.*   John 1:29

If sickness came in through sin (and it did), then how that sin is dealt with is how that sickness must be dealt with too:

> *And, behold, they brought to him a man sick of the palsy, lying on a bed: and Jesus seeing their faith said unto the sick*

of the palsy; Son, be of good cheer; thy
sins be forgiven thee.   Matthew 9:2

In the instant Jesus told this man, *"Son, thy sins be forgiven,"* he was also healed. When Jesus dealt with the sin, the diseases naturally followed. In Jesus, you are free from every attack of sickness and disease.

If, by the power of the blood of Jesus Christ, God could no more see sin, then disease also must be a thing of the past.

Jesus said to His followers, *"In my name, heal the sick":*

Heal the sick, cleanse the lepers, raise
the dead, cast out devils: freely ye have
received, freely give.   Matthew 10:8

We can minister healing to others by God's power because He *"put away sin by the sacrifice of Himself":*

For then must he often have suffered
since the foundation of the world: but
now once in the end of the world hath he

appeared to put away sin by the sacrifice
of himself.   Hebrews 9:26

We must break loose from casual living and
religious dogma, and we can do that because
the Creator, the living God, dwells in us. You
and I were destined to live by miracles.

The world has been deceived, but you
and I have the answers the world needs. As
Proverbs declares:

> *Many are the plans in the mind of a*
> *man, but it is the purpose of the* Lord
> *that will stand.* Proverbs 19:21, ESV

One important part of God's plan for mankind is to live in health. He said:

> *Beloved, I wish above all things that*
> *thou mayest prosper and be in health,*
> *even as thy soul prospereth.*   3 John 2

There is a yearning within each of us to
fulfill God's plans, but without having good
health, that plan is in jeopardy. We must

insist on receiving what is ours and putting the devil out of business:

And a great multitude followed him, because they saw his miracles which he did on them that were diseased.

John 6:2

Whosoever denieth the Son, the same hath not the Father: he that acknowledgeth the Son hath the Father also.

1 John 2:23

Our redemption is incomplete without the demonstration of miracles in our daily lives. When we believe and step into the realm of God and His manifest love, it proves to everyone around us that not only is Jesus Christ alive, but also that He is the same yesterday, today, and forever:

Jesus Christ the same yesterday, and to day, and for ever. Hebrews 13:8

103

God has already declared clearly that He is your Healer:

> *He said, "If you will listen carefully to the voice of the Lord your God and do what is right in his sight, obeying his commands and keeping all his decrees, then I will not make you suffer any of the diseases I sent on the Egyptians; for I am the Lord who heals you.*
> Exodus 15:26, NLT

Your destiny is God's pride. As a redeemed child of God, you are not expected to live a defeated and miserable life. The price God was willing to pay to redeem you shows the value He puts on your life. We were not redeemed by perishable or corruptible things like gold and silver:

> *Forasmuch as ye know that ye were not redeemed with corruptible things, as silver and gold, from your vain conversation received by tradition from your fathers; but with the precious blood of*

*Christ, as of a lamb without blemish and
without spot.*   1 Peter 1:18-19

God's own life was the price paid to free
you from all limitations, sicknesses, and perils of life. That's what we mean by the grace
of God. It brings revolution, transformation,
favor, blessing, and unending peace and
power. And it's all because of the finished
work of Christ on the cross:

> *To me, though I am the very least of all
> the saints (God's consecrated people),
> this grace (favor, privilege) was granted
> and graciously entrusted: to proclaim to
> the Gentiles the unending (boundless,
> fathomless, incalculable, and exhaust-
> less) riches of Christ [wealth which no
> human being could have searched out].*
>   Ephesians 3:8, AMPC

> *Yet we know that a person is made right
> with God by faith in Jesus Christ, not by
> obeying the law. And we have believed
> in Christ Jesus, so that we might be*

made right with God because of our faith in Christ, not because we have obeyed the law. For no one will ever be made right with God by obeying the law.
Galatians 2:16, NLT

And [Jesus] came and preached peace to you which were afar off, and to them that were nigh. For through him we both have access by one Spirit unto the Father. Ephesians 2:17-18

We have not been brought near to God through something we have done, but only through the precious blood of Jesus Christ:

But now in Christ Jesus ye who sometimes were far off are made nigh by the blood of Christ. Ephesians 2:13

As a result, we now live in an atmosphere of productivity and results, and we must not allow ourselves to be cheated. Your complete forgiveness puts you on a level with God, divine elevation making you a star to watch:

The Jews answered him, saying, For a good work we stone thee not; but for blasphemy; and because that thou, being a man, makest thyself God.

Jesus answered them, Is it not written in your law, I said, Ye are gods? If he called them gods, unto whom the word of God came, and the scripture cannot be broken; say ye of him, whom the Father hath sanctified, and sent into the world, Thou blasphemest; because I said, I am the Son of God?   John 10:33-36

For I will be merciful to their unrighteousness, and their sins and their iniquities will I remember no more.
Hebrews 8:12

This is why God presents you to Himself a Church without wrinkle, spot, or blemish:

That he might sanctify and cleanse it with the washing of water by the word, that he might present it to himself a glorious church, not having spot, or wrinkle, or any such thing; but that it should be holy and without blemish.

Ephesians 5:26-27

It was religion, culture, and tradition that brought fear into Christianity, along with condemnation, guilt, lack of faith, and doubt. God gave us His standard:

There is therefore now no condemnation to them which are in Christ Jesus, who walk not after the flesh, but after the Spirit. For the law of the Spirit of life in Christ Jesus hath made me free from the law of sin and death.

Romans 8:1-2

The God who should condemn you justifies you and makes intercession for you:

Who is he that condemneth? It is Christ that died, yea rather, that is risen again, who is even at the right hand of God, who also maketh intercession for us.

Romans 8:34

God is not in the business of condemn-ing anyone; He is out to save men and women, boys and girls and bring them into His Kingdom. This could only be achieved through Jesus' death:

> *For God sent not his Son into the world to condemn the world; but that the world through him might be saved.* John 3:17

It is not your filthiness and sin that keep you from Jesus; it is your lack of under-standing of how much He really loves you.

GOD'S STRENGTH FOR YOUR WEAKNESS

> *And one of them smote the servant of the high priest, and cut off his right ear. And Jesus answered and said, Suffer ye thus far. And he touched his ear, and healed him.* Luke 22:50-51

As we have seen, men came to arrest Jesus. In fact, there were some six hundred soldiers and temple policemen. And, along with them came the servant of the High Priest. He just happened to be Jesus' number one enemy. His name was Malcus.

One of the reasons for the hatred they had for Jesus was that He performed miracles. They were Sadducees and, as such, they didn't believe in the supernatural, the resurrection, or miracles.

In the intensity of the emotions of the moment, Peter took the law into his hands and cut off the man's ear. Then Jesus stepped in and healed the ear. He loved even those who hated Him and wanted Him dead.

In that moment, Peter was weak, but Jesus was strong. Wherever there is weakness in your life, I decree strength today in Jesus' name.

The woman at the well was dirty. She had gone through a lot of divorces, and was experiencing the shame and guilt of it all. But Jesus even passed up His meal to speak with her. He knew her inside and out, and yet He chose to reveal Himself to her.

This woman was a Samaritan, and the law of the day was that Jews should not even speak to Samaritans. Yet Jesus reached out to her. The great I AM is not about your faults, but, rather, about turning things around if we will but allow Him to do it. Your sense of guilt may be fed by pride because you think you can fix it without God's help. You can't:

> *There cometh a woman of Samaria to draw water: Jesus saith unto her, Give me to drink. (For his disciples were gone away unto the city to buy meat.) Then saith the woman of Samaria unto him, How is it that thou, being a Jew, askest drink of me, which am a woman of Samaria? for the Jews have no dealings with the Samaritans.*
>
> *Jesus answered and said unto her, If thou knewest the gift of God, and who it is that saith to thee, Give me to drink; thou wouldest have asked of him, and he would have given thee living water. ...*
>
> *In the mean while his disciples prayed him, saying, Master, eat.*

111

But he said unto them, I have meat to eat that ye know not of.

Therefore said the disciples one to another, Hath any man brought him ought to eat?

Jesus saith unto them, My meat is to do the will of him that sent me, and to finish his work.

John 4:7-10 and 31-34

Have you ever considered how serious Peter's denial of Jesus was? He not only denied Jesus three times; he swore he didn't even know Him. But when Jesus rose from the dead, Peter ran to the tomb. Yes, he was guilty, so how would he face Jesus now, knowing full well that the two of them had an eye contact when he had denied Jesus?

And after a little while another saw him, and said, Thou art also of them. And Peter said, Man, I am not.

And about the space of one hour after another confidently affirmed, saying, Of a truth this fellow also was with him: for he is a Galilaean.

And Peter said, Man, I know not what thou sayest. And immediately, while he yet spake, the cock crew.

And the Lord turned, and looked upon Peter. And Peter remembered the word of the Lord, how he had said unto him, Before the cock crow, thou shalt deny me thrice.

And Peter went out, and wept bitterly.

Luke 22:58-62

Peter ran to Jesus because he knew Jesus was his righteousness, not his judgment. Run back to Him now and receive the strength you need for the journey. He will not reject you:

All that the Father giveth me shall come to me; and him that cometh to me I will in no wise cast out. John 6:37

"I will in no wise cast [you] out." What powerful words! They are still true today.

After Jesus had risen, the disciples went fishing. That was clearly not what He had told them to do before He died. They forsook their divine assignment and concentrated on something to eat. John recorded, *"That night they caught nothing"* (John 21:3). Of course!

And what did Jesus do? He went near to them and called out from the shore, *"Have ye any meat [fish]?"* and they answered, *"No"* (Verse 5).

These men were not doing the right thing, not fulfilling their divine calling, and yet Jesus provided for them. His only words to them when they came ashore and saw who He was were these, *"Come and dine"* (Verse 12). He not only gave them fish but also bread (Verse 13).

Why would Jesus have done this? Because He loved them and His grace pulled them out. Later He reminded Peter, *"Feed my sheep"* (Verse 16). Peter (and, likewise, all the others) was not to allow a job, his daily cares, or any engagement (no matter how important) to take the place of serving Jesus. Nothing must be allowed to push Him out of first place in our lives:

> *Or despisest thou the riches of his goodness and forbearance and longsuffering; not knowing that the goodness of God leadeth thee to repentance?* Romans 2:4

I am blessed, lifted, honored, and highly favored. I decree that Heaven is opened over me now, and I command a release of blessings in the name of Jesus Christ.

Satan, I shut you down as touching my life and destiny.

Father, in the name of Jesus Christ, by the mercies of the living God, I receive divine connection for the fulfillment of my dream.

Yes, we are *Joint Heirs with Christ* and, because of it, the world will see that we are different.

CHAPTER 8

DARE TO BE IN CONTROL OF THE TERRITORY GOD HAS GIVEN YOU

Heaven and earth shall pass away, but my words shall not pass away.

Matthew 24:35

You and I belong to a Kingdom with a template designed for its citizens to take over assigned territories. As citizens of Heaven, we are not subject to the system of this world. Instead, we are empowered to rule over it:

And again he [Jesus] said, Whereunto shall I liken the kingdom of God? It is

*like leaven, which a woman took and hid
in three measures of meal, till the whole
was leavened.* Luke 13:20-21

Blossoming and becoming impactful and resourceful is our mandate here on earth. God wants us to take instructions from Him in order to take our territory and rule it well.

All Peter needed to change his financial status was to launch into the deep at the command of Jesus. The fish were not the problem. God can put as many fish as we need in the sea where there was nothing before.

However there is no taking over territory without a fight. If you are not ready for a fight, then forget about ruling. We all know that every Promised Land is full of giants, and you can never defeat these giants if you have a dwarf or grasshopper mentality. Boldly taking the battle to the gates is what will establish your reign.

In God's Kingdom, it's not normal to be sick, poor, enslaved, or limited. That was not in the original plan. But Giants will not give up simply because you're a Christian; you have to be a fighter.

In writing to the Ephesians, Paul gave the key to victory over Satan:

Neither give place to the devil.

Ephesians 4:27

God has given to us all that pertains to life and godliness (see 2 Peter 1:3), but it takes a fight of faith to gain your portion:

Rise ye up, take your journey, and pass over the river Arnon: behold, I have given into thine hand Sihon the Amorite, king of Heshbon, and his land: begin to possess it, and contend with him in battle. This day will I begin to put the dread of thee and the fear of thee upon the nations that are under the whole heaven, who shall hear report of thee, and shall tremble, and be in anguish because of thee.

Deuteronomy 2:24-25

Paul wrote:

> *For a great door and effectual is opened unto me, and there are many adversaries.*
> 1 Corinthians 16:9

The mandate of Jesus Christ to each of us is this:

OCCUPY TILL I COME!
—Luke 19:13

But what does that mean? It means, "Take territory and hold it for Me." The promises of God for our lives stand, but there are forces that want to make His Word appear to be fake. It is our responsibility to stand our ground and declare exactly what the Word says and means:

> *And I said unto the angel that talked with me, What be these? And he answered me, These are the horns which have scattered Judah, Israel, and Jerusalem.*

119

And the LORD *shewed me four carpen-*
ters. Then said I, What come these to
do?
And he spake, saying, These are the
horns which have scattered Judah, so
that no man did lift up his head: but
these are come to fray them, to cast out
the horns of the Gentiles, which lifted
up their horn over the land of Judah to
scatter it.   Zechariah 1:19-21

The Bible shows us that God has planted
the very best in your life, but the enemy
comes in and sows tares. There are forces
that want to frustrate humanity and pull
people down. These are the thorns. But
Jesus has already given us the victory, and
you can enforce that victory by faith:

Anoither parable put he forth unto
them, saying, The kingdom of heaven is
likened unto a man which sowed good
seed in his field: but while men slept, his
enemy came and sowed tares among the
wheat, and went his way. ...

He said unto them, An enemy hath done this. The servants said unto him, Wilt thou then that we go and gather them up?   Matthew 13:24-25 and 28

There were many prophecies concerning the birth of Jesus Christ, so that His coming to earth was real and established. He was indeed born, but early on Herod wanted Him dead at all costs. And this is exactly how the enemy determines to destroy our lives, our visions, and our destinies. If nothing is done about it, what the enemy has determined may as well come to pass.

Because of Herod's plot to kill Jesus, many other children were killed. Herod wanted no competition to his glory, and was willing to sacrifice the lives of many to achieve his purpose. Because of it, many precious lives were cut short, many destinies aborted. Eventually, for the assignment of Jesus to thrive, Herod had to die:

Arise, and take the young child and his mother, and go into the land of Israel: for

> *they are dead which sought the young*
> *child's life.* Matthew 2:20

Whatever has been set to destroy the glory and dream God gave you is cut off now in the name of Jesus Christ!

It's quite unfortunate that despite the fact that God has shown us the way out, many decide to make their own way in the world. Of course, they never get anywhere. Jesus said, *"One thing is needful"*:

> *But one thing is needful: and Mary hath*
> *chosen that good part, which shall not*
> *be taken away from her.* Luke 10:42

What was that one needful thing? The Word of God is our key to stardom and effectiveness. It is through the promises of God that we can have the divine nature to take over:

> *Whereby are given unto us exceeding*
> *great and precious promises: that by these*

ye might be partakers of the divine nature,
having escaped the corruption that is in
the world through lust.   2 Peter 1:4

The land has already been given to us, but we must take up our weapons and divine equipment and fight to take our lawful inheritance.

Beloved, the picture the world has of the Church must change. God did not intend it as the world sees it. In early Christianity, when there was famine, all the believers sent help to those in need:

> *And there stood up one of them named*
> *Agabus, and signified by the Spirit that*
> *there should be great dearth throughout*
> *all the world: which came to pass in the*
> *days of Claudius Caesar. Then the dis-*
> *ciples, every man according to his ability,*
> *determined to send relief unto the brethren*
> *which dwelt in Judaea.*   Acts 11:28-29

Even though Nicodemus was an acade-mician, he did not have an answer to the questions of life. A centurion also came to Jesus Christ to find answers to his questions. Today, we, too, often foolishly endeavor to do things in our own strength, trying to move forward without the consciousness of God's presence all around us and in us. This presence of God with us and in us is the guarantee that we will come out on top:

> *There was a man of the Pharisees, named Nicodemus, a ruler of the Jews: the same came to Jesus by night, and said unto him, Rabbi, we know that thou art a teacher come from God: for no man can do these miracles that thou doest, except God be with him.*
>
> *Jesus answered and said unto him, Verily, verily, I say unto thee, Except a man be born again, he cannot see the kingdom of God. ...*
>
> *The wind bloweth where it listeth, and thou hearest the sound thereof, but canst not tell whence it cometh, and whither it goeth: so is every one that is born of the Spirit.* John 3:1-3 and 8

Once we are born again, we can come to the same level of operations as Jesus. That gives us the audacity we need to destroy the works of the devil and build God's Kingdom. You must be spiritually minded to take over. You are destined to be a lender, not a borrower. Know your status in Christ and move up to the next level.

Satan, the thief, has stolen from us, and we must get it back:

> *Men do not despise a thief, if he steal to satisfy his soul when he is hungry; but if he be found, he shall restore sevenfold; he shall give all the substance of his house.* Proverbs 6:30-31

The problem is this: many want to be strong in the Lord and rule their universe, but they are not strong in His Word, and you cannot be strong in the Lord without faith (which comes from hearing and knowing the Word):

> *Finally, my brethren, be strong in the Lord, and in the power of his might. Put*

on the whole armour of God, that ye may be able to stand against the wiles of the devil. For we wrestle not against flesh and blood, but against principalities, against powers, against the rulers of the darkness of this world, against spiritual wickedness in high places.

Wherefore take unto you the whole armour of God, that ye may be able to withstand in the evil day, and having done all, to stand. Stand therefore, having your loins girt about with truth, and having on the breastplate of righteousness; and your feet shod with the preparation of the gospel of peace; above all, taking the shield of faith, wherewith ye shall be able to quench all the fiery darts of the wicked. And take the helmet of salvation, and the sword of the Spirit, which is the word of God: praying always with all prayer and supplication in the Spirit, and watching thereunto with all perseverance and supplication for all saints.

Ephesians 6:10-18

And being not weak in faith, he [Abraham] considered not his own body now dead, when he was about an hundred years old, neither yet the deadness of Sarah's womb: he staggered not at the promise of God through unbelief; but was strong in faith, giving glory to God; and being fully persuaded that, what he had promised, he was able also to perform. Romans 4:19-21

What demons want us to believe is that our faith is not working. They bring discouragement, fear, and dissatisfaction. Jesus told Peter, *"Satan hath desired to have you"*:

And the Lord said, Simon, Simon, behold, Satan hath desired to have you, that he may sift you as wheat: but I have prayed for thee, that thy faith fail not: and when thou art converted, strengthen thy brethren. Luke 22:31-32

Our battles are not physical, but the effects are obvious. The Bible says that Satan deceived David into numbering the children of Israel. Why? His motive was to make this young man depend on his own strength and move away from God. Satan's mission, as we know, is *"to steal, and to kill, and to destroy"* (John 10:10). Peter described Satan as being *"as a roaring lion, seeking whom he might devour"* (1 Peter 5:8). How can we protect ourselves?

> *And when the tempter came to him [Jesus], he said, If thou be the Son of God, command that these stones be made bread. But he answered and said, It is written, Man shall not live by bread alone, but by every word that proceedeth out of the mouth of God.* Matthew 4:3-4

You have the authority of the name of Jesus Christ, and you have the authority of the blood of Jesus Christ, and you have the authority of God's Word. Force the devil out now, and let the name of Jesus be glorified. You are due for a new level. All you need for a change of story is *"It is written,"* and the forces of darkness are defeated:

*And the LORD said unto Moses, Yet will
I bring one plague more upon Pharaoh,
and upon Egypt; afterwards he will let
you go hence: when he shall let you go,
he shall surely thrust you out hence
altogether.* Exodus 11:1

**Whatever is standing in my way, leave
now. Get out in Jesus' name.**

**Father, in the name of Jesus Christ and
by the blood of Jesus Christ, I destroy
the operations of the evil one in my life
today.**

**Father, in the name of Jesus Christ,
throughout the coming days I forbid
sickness, disease, and lack in my life.**

Yes, we are *Joint Heirs with Christ* and,
because of it, the world will see that we are
different.

CHAPTER 9

WAKE UP!
WISDOM IS YOUR KEY

My people are destroyed for lack of knowledge: because thou hast rejected knowledge, I will also reject thee, that thou shalt be no priest to me: seeing thou hast forgotten the law of thy God, I will also forget thy children. Hosea 4:6

Every frustration and affliction in the Body of Christ is tied to ignorance, not to the devil. When Jesus cried on the cross, *"It is finished"* (John 19:30), it signified to the devil, "Hands off of My saints." Why? Because all power belonged to Jesus Christ:

And Jesus came and spake unto them, saying, All power is given unto me in heaven and in earth.   Matthew 28:18

That same power is given to the saints of God today:

And the kingdom and dominion, and the greatness of the kingdom under the whole heaven, shall be given to the people of the saints of the most High, whose kingdom is an everlasting kingdom, and all dominions shall serve and obey him.   Daniel 7:27

This is what God intended. Sadly, many of His people are in captivity for lack of knowledge of His truths:

Therefore my people are gone into captivity, because they have no knowledge: and their honourable men are famished, and their multitude dried up with thirst.   Isaiah 5:13

Without the knowledge of God, there can be no wisdom of God, and without the wisdom of God, you cannot take control of your world. The Bible shows us very clearly *"wisdom and knowledge shall be the stability of thy times and strength of salvation"*:

> *And wisdom and knowledge shall be the stability of thy times, and strength of salvation: the fear of the LORD is his treasure.* Isaiah 33:6

Just knowing what the Bible says is not enough. We must say what He is saying and act in accordance. Mary, the mother of Jesus, said to those in charge at a marriage in Cana of Galilee, *"Whatsoever he saith unto you, do it"* (John 2:5). They obeyed, and Jesus' first public miracle was the result. Obedience is the key to your miracle too.

Jesus knew His destiny:

> *And as they were afraid, and bowed down their faces to the earth, they said unto them, Why seek ye the living*

among the dead? He is not here, but is risen: remember how he spake unto you when he was yet in Galilee, saying, The Son of man must be delivered into the hands of sinful men, and be crucified, and the third day rise again.

Luke 24:5-7

Today, say something about your destiny as you see it in the Word of God. For instance, say, *"I am the head and not the tail. I am above only and not beneath."* You can say that based on God's promise in Deuteronomy 28:13:

> *And the* Lord *shall make thee the head, and not the tail; and thou shalt be above only, and thou shalt not be beneath; if that thou hearken unto the commandments of the* Lord *thy God, which I command thee this day, to observe and to do them.*

When you say this, mean it, and that will be wisdom for your daily life. It's not enough just to be saved. After you're saved, you need to know what to do to fulfill God's unique plan for your life.

Whenever you see poverty, lack, oppression, or confusion in your life, it is often based on a lack of wisdom and not any particular act of Satan. The disciples were commanded to feed the five thousand, but how to begin? What to do first? Jesus knew what to do, and He told them step by step. When they followed His simple guidance, everyone was fed, and plenty of food was left over.

Knowing what to do is wisdom. I release the wisdom of God for great results upon your life now in Jesus' name.

The Church is designed to show the world what God looks like, and this can be accomplished by demonstrating His wisdom for optimum results.

When you are born again, you become a spirit being living in a physical body, and the Spirit of God dwells in you. That Spirit is far and away more intelligent than your brain. The Spirit of God knows all things:

But God hath revealed them unto us by his Spirit: for the Spirit searcheth all things, yea, the deep things of God.

1 Corinthians 2:10

As a believer in Jesus Christ, you cannot be stranded in this life. You have a great purpose, a great destiny.

Again, there is a wrong perception of the Church by the world. It's really a deception, a trick of the devil to make people lose interest in what is important. The Church is the answer to the world's questions:

Howbeit we speak wisdom among them that are perfect: yet not the wisdom of this world, nor of the princes of this world, that come to nought: but we speak the wisdom of God in a mystery, even the hidden wisdom, which God ordained before the world unto our glory: which none of the princes of this world knew: for had they known it, they would not have crucified the Lord of glory.

1 Corinthians 2:6-8

135

When we use God's approach to any issue, we will beat the world hands down. God's intention was for man to dominate and subdue the earth and be fruitful or productive. The only way to do this is through His wisdom:

> *The Lord by wisdom hath founded the earth; by understanding hath he established the heavens.* Proverbs 3:19

All of Creation was based on the simple words, *"And God said."* And when God said it, it happened. Therefore, the Word of God is His wisdom. We have that same tool, so you can begin to create your world today:

> *I was chosen to explain to everyone this mysterious plan that God, the Creator of all things, had kept secret from the beginning. God's purpose in all this was to use the church to display his wisdom in its rich variety to all the unseen rulers and authorities in the heavenly places.* Ephesians 3:9-10, NLT

God's wisdom is a spirit, and when He rests upon you, you will know the answer to the questions of life. It was the Spirit of wisdom that gave Daniel a place at the top. He went from slavery to mastery:

> *Then this Daniel was preferred above the presidents and princes, because an excellent spirit was in him; and the king thought to set him over the whole realm.* Daniel 6:3

"An excellent spirit was in him."

You can't have divine wisdom and not see mighty works. The people of Jesus' day said of Him:

> *What wisdom is this which is given unto him, that even such mighty works are wrought by his hands?* Mark 6:2

The master blueprint for doing things is using a heavenly formula to solve earthly issues. Jesus told His confused disciples to first have the people sit down in companies:

*And Jesus took the loaves; and when he
had given thanks, he distributed to the
disciples, and the disciples to them that
were set down; and likewise of the fishes
as much as they would. When they were
filled, he said unto his disciples, Gather
up the fragments that remain, that nothing be lost. Therefore they gathered them
together, and filled twelve baskets with
the fragments of the five barley loaves,
which remained over and above unto
them that had eaten.*   John 6:11-13

Next, Jesus gave thanks for the bread and
fish and blessed them:

*And when he had taken the five loaves
and the two fishes, he looked up to heav-
en, and blessed, and brake the loaves,
and gave them to his disciples to set
before them; and the two fishes divided
he among them all.*   Verse 41

It is wisdom to give thanks when what
you have is not enough. Then God stepped
in with multiplication:

And they did all eat, and were filled. And they took up twelve baskets full of the fragments, and of the fishes. And they that did eat of the loaves were about five thousand men. Verses 42-44

It all started with wisdom, and the entire process was stress free and powerful.

The wisdom to honor our elders leads to long life:

Children, obey your parents in the Lord: for this is right. Honour thy father and mother; which is the first commandment with promise; that it may be well with thee, and thou mayest live long on the earth. Ephesians 6:1-3

Another biblical key to long life is learning to control your tongue:

What man is he that desireth life, and loveth many days, that he may see good? Keep thy tongue from evil, and thy lips

from speaking guile. Depart from evil,
and do good; seek peace, and pursue it.
Psalm 34:12-14

The application of the Scriptures to your daily life also lengthens your stay here:

Therefore whosoever heareth these say-
ings of mine, and doeth them, I will
liken him unto a wise man, which built
his house upon a rock. Matthew 7:24

Wisdom is crying out in the street:

Wisdom crieth without; she uttereth her
voice in the streets. Proverbs 1:20

Get connected to wisdom, and you will succeed and enjoy long life.

Yes, we are *Joint Heirs with Christ* and, because of it, the world will see that we are different.

CHAPTER 10

HOW TO GET WISDOM

And the child [Jesus] grew, and waxed strong in spirit, filled with wisdom: and the grace of God was upon him.   Luke 2:40

And Jesus increased in wisdom and stature, and in favour with God and man.   Luke 2:52

Even Jesus needed wisdom, and He began to demonstrate it very early in life. If wisdom was that important to Jesus, how much more do we need it today. Having wisdom is part of our co-heritage with Christ, but how do we acquire wisdom?

THROUGH THE WORD OF GOD

My son, if thou wilt receive my words, and hide my commandments with thee; so that thou incline thine ear unto wisdom, and apply thine heart to understanding; yea, if thou criest after knowledge, and liftest up thy voice for understanding; if thou seekest her as silver, and searchest for her as for hid treasures; then shalt thou understand the fear of the LORD, and find the knowledge of God. For the LORD giveth wisdom: out of his mouth cometh knowledge and understanding.

Proverbs 2:1-6

Your access to divine wisdom is the written Word of God. His Word is loaded with nuggets of God's wisdom. Read the Word and meditate upon it regularly.

THROUGH READING GOOD BOOKS AND LISTENING TO ANOINTED RECORDINGS

God's wisdom has been imparted to men and women through the centuries, and we can benefit from their experience by reading their books and listening to their anointed teachings. But seek God about what you read and listen to. Not every book or every recording is according to God's Word, the Holy Bible. If it strays from His Word, it is not inspired by Him.

Too many times, we are bound up in an old way of doing things and can't see beyond it. The questions of life can have new answers.

When David wanted to fight Goliath, everyone told him it had never been done. Goliath had been a warrior from his youth, and it was quite true that no one had ever killed a giant with a sling. But David was not moved by these arguments. Maybe it had never been done before, but he knew how God had helped him kill a lion and a bear. What had never been done could start with him.

God has called each of us to break barriers and challenge boundaries, and the faith to do it can come by reading good books and listening to anointed teachings. We are not destined to become stranded in life. Whatever has not yet existed can be created by God's Word:

> *In the beginning was the Word, and the Word was with God, and the Word was God. The same was in the beginning with God. All things were made by him; and without him was not any thing made that was made.* John 1:1-3

This is the power that was with God from the beginning. Nothing existed without the Word. Everything and everyone (even the devil) came by the Word. Satan perverted things that God had created, but God has given us the Word to change everything:

> *In him was life; and the life was the light of men.* John 1:4

Light came by the Word of God, and that's why darkness and evil cannot stand the

Word. Let the Word, spoken or written by men and women of God, inspire and light up your life.

BY THE LAYING ON OF THE HANDS OF THE PROPHETS

Wisdom can be imparted to others because it's a spirit. Knowledge is acquired, but wisdom can be imparted:

> *And Joshua the son of Nun was full of the spirit of wisdom; for Moses had laid his hands upon him: and the children of Israel hearkened unto him, and did as the LORD commanded Moses.*
>
> Deuteronomy 34:9

Paul said

> *For I long to see you, that I may impart unto you some spiritual gift, to the end ye may be established.*   Romans 1:11

BY TRAINING AND MENTORSHIP

Since wisdom can be imparted, the more time we spend under the training and mentorship of godly men and women, the better it will be for us. Again, ask God to guide you and show you who to submit to.

The wisdom you gain from others will make you creative, and if you're not creative, you will end up being a burden. On the other hand, when you celebrate ideas and analyze them, you make your world bow before you, and whatever you celebrate you attract. This was what happened to Zacchaeus (see Luke 19:1-10).

Open yourself to training and mentoring, for it will expand your imagination, and you will become wiser than your equals. Imparted divine wisdom will add value to your daily life.

BY PRAYER

If any of you lack wisdom, let him ask of God, that giveth to all men liberally, and upbraideth not; and it shall be given him. James 1:5

When there is instability, it is often a lack of wisdom, not because you're not saved. Wisdom gives you the ability to control your life and be in charge of your destiny. It manifests in creative imaginations, creative ideas, and the proper management of your time. That's why the Bible states that if you lack wisdom, you should pray. And the promise is: *"IT SHALL BE GIVEN."*

Father, by Your mercy, I receive Your wisdom today. I am on my way to the top. I must win souls in the days to come. My destiny is opened for great results.

Father, I dispel every distraction on my way to the top now in the name of Jesus Christ.

Yes, we are *Joint Heirs with Christ* and, because of it, the world will see that we are different.

CHAPTER 11

GET YOUR THINKING STRAIGHT

Come now, and let us reason together, saith the LORD: though your sins be as scarlet, they shall be as white as snow; though they be red like crimson, they shall be as wool. If ye be willing and obedient, ye shall eat the good of the land. Isaiah 1:18-19

Never forget that your level of influence and the results you will have are determined by your level of thinking, not just your praying. The good is in the land, but it takes proper reasoning to find it:

For as he thinketh in his heart, so is he: Eat and drink, saith he to thee; but his heart is not with thee. Proverbs 23:7

It is amazing that what puts you on top is residing within you. When your thinking is not right, it affects your living. Why? Because your thinking affects your believing. The reason we are given the mind of Christ is to reason like Him and become creative in order to amaze our world:

For who hath known the mind of the Lord, that he may instruct him? but we have the mind of Christ.
1 Corinthians 2:16

You are not ordinary, and yet the world will try to reduce you to a nobody by conditioning your mind to its mold. You cannot call yourself a grasshopper if you think like a giant. You will see yourself the way you think about yourself.

Your present status is a product of your present level of reasoning, Engaging in productive thinking makes a champion out of even a seeming dummy:

> *Finally, brethren, whatsoever things are true, whatsoever things are honest, whatsoever things are just, whatsoever things are pure, whatsoever things are lovely, whatsoever things are of good report; if there be any virtue, and if there be any praise, think on these things.*
>
> Philippians 4:8

You were not designed to fail and live like a commoner, but you can make a choice to do so, and no one will be able to change that:

> *Say unto them, As truly as I live, saith the* LORD, *as ye have spoken in mine ears, so will I do to you.*
>
> Numbers 14:28

Why is this true? Because out of the abundance of the heart the mouth speaks. You speak what you think:

O generation of vipers, how can ye, being evil, speak good things? for out of the abundance of the heart the mouth speaketh.   Matthew 12:34

What life brings your way is not nearly as important as the way you respond to it:

When thou goest out to battle against thine enemies, and seest horses, and chariots, and a people more than thou, be not afraid of them: for the LORD thy God is with thee, which brought thee up out of the land of Egypt. Deuteronomy 20:1

The compassionate love of Christ will never allow you to crash and be drowned, no matter what.

As the Father hath loved me, so have I loved you: continue ye in my love.
                                        John 15:9

The wise and the foolish face the same ordeals, but the wise make a choice to stand on the Word of Christ, and as a result, they cannot be shaken. They're not lucky, as some have thought. They just make better choices.

When your choice is made, God is committed to it. The Hebrew boys who were caught up in the fiery furnace said:

> *Our God whom we serve is able to deliver us from the burning fiery furnace, and he will deliver us out of thine hand, O king. But if not, be it known unto thee, O king, that we will not serve thy gods, nor worship the golden image which thou hast set up.*
>
> Daniel 3:17-18

Of course this infuriated the king, but their decision saved them:

> *And the princes, governors, and captains, and the king's counsellors, being gathered together, saw these men, upon whose bodies the fire had no power, nor was an hair of their head singed, neither*

were their coats changed, nor the smell of fire had passed on them. Daniel 3:27

These men saw the Almighty as bigger and stronger than the fire, and so they refused to bow. If you refuse to bow, you will also be a winner.

Paul wrote: *"Let the word of Christ dwell in you richly in all wisdom":*

> *Let the word of Christ dwell in you richly in all wisdom; teaching and admonishing one another in psalms and hymns and spiritual songs, singing with grace in your hearts to the Lord.*
> Colossians 3:16

This is the key that will sustain you when others have failed. The key to sustainable change is right thinking. Change the way you think, and you will change the way you live:

> *For as he thinketh in his heart, so is he.*
> Proverbs 23:7

Only five percent of our population is wealthy and victorious. Why are they different? Because they are thinking differently. They have faced challenges too, but they overcame. You were designed to live in abundance and affluence ... if you can only allow your mind to catch up with God's plan. He said clearly:

> *For I know the thoughts that I think toward you, saith the* LORD, *thoughts of peace, and not of evil, to give you an expected end.*   Jeremiah 29:11

Abundance and affluence don't often come overnight, but consistency is the rule of the game. Jesus showed that when we have gifts and talents, we must invest them, not hide them for safekeeping. If we are not investing, putting to use what God has given us, we are wasting valuable resources.

It is not your savings that makes you rich; it's your investments. Money is a tool to invest, not just a way of getting things. It is best to buy things out of abundance, not out of lack. Wealth is an idea, not money.

Make investing a priority, and you will indeed invest. The rich are always thinking about investments, while the poor are always looking for a better job. Too many are interested in maintenance, not abundance.

There are gifts and talents inside of every one of us, but not many are truly investing what they have. God wants you to take over, to start thinking right, to get a plan in place, and then to pursue that plan. God directs our steps, not our sits.

GET THE VISION IN PLACE

A vision is about a destination. Do you have a vision for your tithes, a vision about your offerings, a vision about your gifts to God? Do you have a vision concerning your net worth? The level of your thinking determines the level of your production.

God is only involved in wealth that changes lives, and only risk-takers emerge as winners. If you never try anything, you will never become anything. When you know you don't have all the answers, someone will be sent to help you out, and you won't remain in mediocrity. God takes pleasure in your prosperity when you delight yourself in Him, but without commitment, you kill the dream:

> *He that hath no rule over his own spirit*
> *is like a city that is broken down, and*
> *without walls.* Proverbs 25:28

Setting boundaries takes care of your vision. Stop wasteful habits and invest that money instead.

HOW TO DEVELOP CREATIVE THINKING.

Let the Word of God be the basis of your thinking:

> *Therefore whosoever heareth these say-*
> *ings of mine, and doeth them, I will*
> *liken him unto a wise man, which built*

his house upon a rock: and the rain descended, and the floods came, and the winds blew, and beat upon that house; and it fell not: for it was founded upon a rock. Matthew 7:24-25

Don't use formulas; use biblical principles. Formulas are specific fixed guidelines toward an action, but principles are truths that are flexible, depending on the situation. It is not all in knowing what the Bible says; it's doing what the Bible says that forms the foundation for you taking over.

Both the successful and the unsuccessful have formulas for building, but the wise base their lives on principles. Both the wise and the foolish experience storms, but the wise rule over those storms. What about you?

What does God have to say about the subject you're facing? Health? Finances? Relationships, etc.? Do what He says, and stand firm on your decision, and you will prevail.

Never rely on what the devil says:

Now it came to pass on a certain day, that he went into a ship with his disciples: and he said unto them, Let us go over unto the other side of the lake. And they launched forth. But as they sailed he fell asleep: and there came down a storm of wind on the lake; and they were filled with water, and were in jeopardy. And they came to him, and awoke him, saying, Master, master, we perish.
Then he arose, and rebuked the wind and the raging of the water: and they ceased, and there was a calm. And he said unto them, Where is your faith?
And they being afraid wondered, saying one to another, What manner of man is this! for he commandeth even the winds and water, and they obey him.

Luke 8:22-25

Never forget that our forefathers, Adam and Eve, lost their position by listening to the devil. In His time on earth, Jesus Christ reigned supreme by rejecting Satan's words. Satan will test your faith too, trying to stop you from moving on up. Deal with him by the Word of God, just as Jesus did:

And God blessed them, and God said unto them, Be fruitful, and multiply, and replenish the earth, and subdue it: and have dominion over the fish of the sea, and over the fowl of the air, and over every living thing that moveth upon the earth. Genesis 1:28

And the Lord said, If ye had faith as a grain of mustard seed, ye might say unto this sycamine tree, Be thou plucked up by the root, and be thou planted in the sea; and it should obey you. Luke 17:6

Why do we need to subdue and dominate the earth? There are forces that want to take the earth from you, to rob you of your position here. But if you stand strong, nothing can stand in your way, not even a mountain.

So, never stoop to beg. Command the evil forces to leave in Jesus' name, and they will.

There is a principle in Matthew 16 that we all need to employ:

> *And Jesus answered and said unto him, Blessed art thou, Simon Barjona: for flesh and blood hath not revealed it unto thee, but my Father which is in heaven. And I say also unto thee, That thou art Peter, and upon this rock I will build my church; and the gates of hell shall not prevail against it. And I will give unto thee the keys of the kingdom of heaven: and whatsoever thou shalt bind on earth shall be bound in heaven: and whatsoever thou shalt loose on earth shall be loosed in heaven.* Matthew 16:17-19

Are you using the keys you have been given?

Let the questions you face be the foundation for your thinking, not a challenge that poses a problem.

The quality of your questions will determine the quality of your life. You will never have questions if you are content with where you are in life.

David asked:

> *Who is this uncircumcised Philistine, that he should defy the armies of the living God?* 1 Samuel 17:26

His question then provoked a solution. When you ask the right questions, you can't be intimidated. But if there is no question, you limit yourself.

The prodigal son asked:

> *How many hired servants of my father's have bread enough and to spare, and I perish with hunger! I will arise and go to my father.* Luke 15:17-18

This reasoned question led to a reasoned response, and we all know the rest of the story. Are you asking the right questions?

Develop a picture that will enhance creative thinking.

> *And a certain woman, which had an issue of blood twelve years, and had suffered many things of many physicians, and had spent all that she had, and was nothing bettered, but rather grew worse, when she had heard of Jesus, came in the press behind, and touched his garment. For she said, If I may touch but his clothes, I shall be whole. And straightway the fountain of her blood was dried up; and she felt in her body that she was healed of that plague.*   Mark 5:25-29

This woman with the issue of blood was looking for God's healing wings, for she knew His covenant promises:

> *Speak unto the children of Israel, and bid them that they make them fringes in the borders of their garments throughout their generations, and that they put*

upon the fringe of the borders a ribband of blue. Numbers 15:38

But unto you that fear my name shall the Sun of righteousness arise with healing in his wings; and ye shall go forth, and grow up as calves of the stall. Malachi 4:2

As the positive image on the inside of her changed, the woman changed what she was saying, and it brought deliverance. Let your imagination go to work right now. Where do you desire to be this time next year? Get that picture working. See yourself at the top.

In the name of Jesus Christ, I receive strength and grace by the help of the Holy Ghost to think creatively.

Yes, we are *Joint Heirs with Christ* and, because of it, the world will see that we are different.

163

CHAPTER 12

REFUSE TO BE STRANDED

For by him were all things created, that are in heaven, and that are in earth, visible and invisible, whether they be thrones, or dominions, or principalities, or powers: all things were created by him, and for him: and he is before all things, and by him all things consist.

Colossians 1:16-17

Beloved, you cannot belonged to Jesus Christ and be stranded in life. He is the author of life:

When Christ, who is our life, shall appear, then shall ye also appear with him in glory. Colossians 3:4

Christ Jesus has preeminence in all things, and by Him all things consist. Wake up! All things are yours in Christ!

> *Therefore let no man glory in men. For all things are your's; whether Paul, or Apollos, or Cephas, or the world, or life, or death, or things present, or things to come; all are yours.*
>
> 1 Corinthians 3:21-22

You must be conscious that God is always with you, that He owns all things, and by the virtue of your new birth, this means all things now belong to you by inheritance. Jesus Himself said:

> *All things that the Father hath are mine: therefore said I, that he shall take of mine, and shall shew it unto you.*
>
> John 16:15

You only have what He has shown you by faith. The power of the Word puts an end to all the activities of darkness. The light He produces overcomes all darkness. Darkness cannot extinguish light. Never! But the world around us is filled with darkness and wickedness:

> *And we know that we are of God, and the whole world lieth in wickedness.*
>
> 1 John 5:19

When you see the manifestation of darkness, let the light in you shine forth and dispel it:

> *The Word gave life to everything that was created,*
> *and his life brought light to everyone.*
> *The light shines in the darkness,*
> *and the darkness can never extinguish it.* John 1:4-5, NLT

> *The people which sat in darkness saw great light; and to them which sat in the region and shadow of death light is sprung up.* Matthew 4:16

Good success is possible for anyone with God. Nothing and no one can tamper with His plans, and nothing and no one can limit His glory. He is God:

> *Know therefore this day, and consider it in thine heart, that the LORD he is God in heaven above, and upon the earth beneath: there is none else.*
>
> Deuteronomy 4:39

When Joshua was facing the hosts of the Amalekites and Canaanites, God said to him, "No matter what stands against you, your success is assured." How was that possible? God had said:

> *This book of the law shall not depart out of thy mouth; but thou shalt meditate therein day and night, that thou mayest observe to do according to all that is written therein: for then thou shalt make thy way prosperous, and then thou shalt have good success.* Joshua 1:8

Without mediation on the Word, you cannot see its truths manifest in your life. God does not have an issue with blessing and healing and making life the best for His children. We are born out of His love. But the children of God must be ready to believe, obey, and speak His Word. Jesus said, *"All things are possible"*:

> *Jesus said unto him, If thou canst believe, all things are possible to him that believeth.* Mark 9:23

What God says to you may not make sense. Just believe it and act on it, and it will come to pass.

Jesus healed a blind man by spitting on some clay, anointing those blind eyes with the mud and telling the man to go wash it off. That didn't make any sense at all, but the man came back seeing.

If you will believe God today, you will never again be stranded. But you can't build your shield of faith without utilizing the Word of God. His Word is the surety, a guarantee that He is in it, and He backs it up. Arrows are flying at you every day and everywhere, but your shield of faith built on the Word of God will dispel them:

Above all, taking the shield of faith, wherewith ye shall be able to quench all the fiery darts of the wicked.

Ephesians 6:16

So then faith cometh by hearing, and hearing by the word of God.

Romans 10:17

God's Word is proven and can never fail:

Every place that the sole of your foot shall tread upon, that have I given unto you, as I said unto Moses. Joshua 1:3

God made Joshua to know that the giants in the land were nothing to worry about, that their huge size had nothing to do with their strength. The One who was with him would swallow them up.

Faith quenches all the fiery darts of the devil, not all the goodness of God. The Lord Jesus Christ gave us the Word to rule our world, and neglecting it makes you a victim:

> *For verily I say unto you, That whosoever shall say unto this mountain, Be thou removed, and be thou cast into the sea; and shall not doubt in his heart, but shall believe that those things which he saith shall come to pass; he shall have whatsoever he saith.* Mark 11:23

Jesus is the Guarantor of all that is written and promised. Period! The blessing is designed to overtake you. That is God's plan, and you cannot live without results:

> *And it shall come to pass, if thou shalt hearken diligently unto the voice of the LORD thy God, to observe and to do all his commandments which I command thee this day, that the LORD thy God will set thee on high above all nations of the earth.* Deuteronomy 28:1

The blessing is what God puts on you to enable you to rule your world:

> *And God blessed them, and God said unto them, Be fruitful, and multiply, and replenish the earth, and subdue it: and have dominion over the fish of the sea, and over the fowl of the air, and over every living thing that moveth upon the earth.* Genesis 1:28

This was the same blessing given to Noah, to Abraham, and now to you:

> *And if ye be Christ's, then are ye Abraham's seed, and heirs according to the promise.* Galatians 3:29

Let the Spirit of God create an atmosphere around your life that looks like Heaven. Jesus said:

> *The words that I speak unto you, they are spirit, and they are life.* John 6:63

171

So, speak life and stop death around you. Activate spiritual forces, setting up the system of the Kingdom and releasing the forces of God's Spirit. Nothing on earth can stop these forces. When you speak God's words, everything must obey you.

This is why we, as believers, must be very careful about what we say. As we have seen, God said:

> *As truly as I live, saith the* Lord, *as ye have spoken in mine ears, so will I do to you.* Numbers 14:28

If you are not speaking, then there is no faith:

> *The heart of the wise teacheth his mouth, and addeth learning to his lips. Pleasant words are as an honeycomb, sweet to the soul, and health to the bones.*
> Proverbs 16:23-24

Your life, your destiny, is in your own hands and at the mercy of your tongue. For some, that is a problem:

Behold, we put bits in the horses' mouths, that they may obey us; and we turn about their whole body. Behold also the ships, which though they be so great, and are driven of fierce winds, yet are they turned about with a very small helm, whithersoever the governor listeth. Even so the tongue is a little member, and boasteth great things. Behold, how great a matter a little fire kindleth! And the tongue is a fire, a world of iniquity: so is the tongue among our members, that it defileth the whole body, and setteth on fire the course of nature; and it is set on fire of hell.

For every kind of beasts, and of birds, and of serpents, and of things in the sea, is tamed, and hath been tamed of mankind: but the tongue can no man tame; it is an unruly evil, full of deadly poison.   James 3:3-8

When we speak contrary to the Word of God, we invite evil and give Satan an opening:

> *And they brought up an evil report of the land which they had searched unto the children of Israel, saying, The land, through which we have gone to search it, is a land that eateth up the inhabitants thereof; and all the people that we saw in it are men of a great stature.* Numbers 13:32

> *Even those men that did bring up the evil report upon the land, died by the plague before the LORD.*
> Numbers 14:37

It was deemed *"an evil report,"* not because what they saw was not real, but because they didn't believe what God had said. Say what God says:

> *For by thy words thou shalt be justified, and by thy words thou shalt be condemned.* Matthew 12:37

This is important. *"By thy words,"* not by the devil. This is a heart issue:

Keep thy heart with all diligence; for out of it are the issues of life. Put away from thee a froward mouth, and perverse lips put far from thee.   Proverbs 4:23-24

He that walketh with wise men shall be wise: but a companion of fools shall be destroyed.   Proverbs 13:20

You have the best seed ever, but until you sow it, it can never grow and produce fruit. Keep sowing the Word of God. It has the potency to give you a great increase. But, as noted, the enemy is always after the Word to make you feel that it sometimes fails:

For this people's heart is waxed gross, and their ears are dull of hearing, and their eyes they have closed; lest at any time they should see with their eyes and hear with their ears, and should under-stand with their heart, and should be converted, and I should heal them.
But blessed are your eyes, for they see: and your ears, for they hear. For verily

175

I say unto you, That many prophets and righteous men have desired to see those things which ye see, and have not seen them; and to hear those things which ye hear, and have not heard them.

Hear ye therefore the parable of the sower. When any one heareth the word of the kingdom, and understandeth it not, then cometh the wicked one, and catcheth away that which was sown in his heart. This is he which received seed by the way side. Matthew 13:15-19

It is the seed that determines the fruit, but it is the soil that determines the growth and the outcome:

The tongue of the wise useth knowledge aright: but the mouth of fools poureth out foolishness. The eyes of the LORD are in every place, beholding the evil and the good. A wholesome tongue is a tree of life: but perverseness therein is a breach in the spirit. ...

A man hath joy by the answer of his mouth: and a word spoken in due season, how good is it!

Proverbs 15:2-4 and 23

The more you speak what God has said, the more you prepare your heart to believe it and receive it.

Yes, we are *Joint Heirs with Christ* and, because of it, the world will see that we are different.

177

CHAPTER 13

JESUS CHRIST, THE NAME ABOVE ALL NAMES

Therefore my people are gone into captivity, because they have no knowledge: and their honourable men are famished, and their multitude dried up with thirst. Isaiah 5:13

As noted, it is a lack of knowledge of the truths of the Word of God that brings chaos and fear to any believer. This lack makes the power of God seem insufficient. Shamefully, the children of Ephraim ran away in the day of battle simply because they were ignorant of Who was with them:

The children of Ephraim, being armed, and carrying bows, turned back in the day of battle. They kept not the covenant of God, and refused to walk in his law.

Psalm 78:9-10

When you know that you know God's Word is true and nothing in the entire Universe can change or alter it, then you are settled, bold, and confident. Without that knowledge, you remain vulnerable to the enemy's attacks.

The Bible states clearly that *"the scripture cannot be broken"*:

He called them gods, unto whom the word of God came, and the scripture cannot be broken. John 10:35

Jesus Himself said:

Heaven and earth shall pass away, but my words shall not pass away.

Matthew 24:35

Whatever Jesus represents always comes out on top. His name—Jesus Christ—is all powerful, all-authoritative, and all-glorious. A name doesn't just get attention; it is attached to the spirit of the bearer and his or her character. A name says a lot about a person, and the name Jesus Christ says a lot about our great God.

The saints of old knew God by names He revealed to them from time to time. For instance, God revealed Himself to Abraham in this way:

> *And when Abram was ninety years old and nine, the LORD appeared to Abram, and said unto him, I am the Almighty God; walk before me, and be thou perfect. And I will make my covenant between me and thee, and will multiply thee exceedingly. And Abram fell on his face: and God talked with him.*
>
> Genesis 17:1-3

The name God gave Abraham on this occasion was El Shaddai, translated into

English here as *"the Almighty."* That was all Abraham needed to know, and it canceled every impossibility in his life.

When God showed up as Jehovah-Rapha in Old Testament times, His people knew that sickness had to flee. It could not stay around when they called upon His name. By New Testament times, the Bible declared:

> *And being found in fashion as a man, he [Jesus] humbled himself, and became obedient unto death, even the death of the cross. Wherefore God also hath highly exalted him, and given him a name which is above every name: that at the name of Jesus every knee should bow, of things in heaven, and things in earth, and things under the earth; and that every tongue should confess that Jesus Christ is Lord, to the glory of God the Father.* Philippians 2:8-11

When Isaiah introduced Jesus thousands of years ago, He called Him both *"a son"* and *"the everlasting Father"*:

For unto us a child is born, unto us a son is given: and the government shall be upon his shoulder: and his name shall be called Wonderful, Counsellor, The mighty God, The everlasting Father, The Prince of Peace. Of the increase of his government and peace there shall be no end, upon the throne of David, and upon his kingdom, to order it, and to establish it with judgment and with justice from henceforth even for ever. The zeal of the LORD of hosts will perform this. Isaiah 9:6-7

The Psalms declare the excellence of His name:

O LORD, our LORD, how excellent is thy name in all the earth! who hast set thy glory above the heavens. Psalm 8:1

At that time, His name was rather mysterious, but we now know Him today. He is Jesus Christ, and the entire Universe pays prompt attention whenever His name is mentioned. John the Revelator wrote:

> *And I saw heaven opened, and behold a white horse; and he that sat upon him was called Faithful and True, and in righteousness he doth judge and make war. His eyes were as a flame of fire, and on his head were many crowns; and he had a name written, that no man knew, but he himself. And he was clothed with a vesture dipped in blood: and his name is called The Word of God. And the armies which were in heaven followed him upon white horses, clothed in fine linen, white and clean. And out of his mouth goeth a sharp sword, that with it he should smite the nations: and he shall rule them with a rod of iron: and he treadeth the winepress of the fierceness and wrath of Almighty God. And he hath on his vesture and on his thigh a name written,*
>
> *KING OF KINGS, AND LORD OF LORDS.*
>
> Revelation 19:11-16

You see, the armies of Heaven followed Him. When His name is invoked in faith, Heaven's armies go into action.

Jesus Christ's Angel led the children of Israel during their journey in the wilderness. God said of this Angel, *"My name is in Him"*:

> *Beware of him, and obey his voice, provoke him not; for he will not pardon your transgressions: for my name is in him.* Exodus 23:21

Because the name Jesus represents His person, He has given us this name to carry His presence with us anywhere and everywhere we go. He said:

> *Lo, I am with you always, even unto the end of the world. Amen.*
> Matthew 28:20

He is with us in the name, and the invocation of this name still brings the manifestation and ministration of angels today:

The name of the LORD is a strong tower;
The righteous run to it and are safe.
Proverbs 18:10, NKJV

The name of Jesus is key to fulfilment, to joy, and to destiny in the life of every believer:

Until now you have asked nothing in My name. Ask, and you will receive, that your joy may be full.   John 16:24, NKJV

The name of Jesus is the key to access all that you desire in life. Let's see what benefits you stand to see manifested through the use of that powerful name.

As an Indorsement:

We all know that an important endorsement can create opportunities. When you are suddenly riding on the wings of powerful individuals, it can remove all your struggles. The name of Jesus Christ is an endorsement for you. He said:

> *And whatever you ask in My name, that*
> *I will do, that the Father may be glorified*
> *in the Son. If you ask anything in My*
> *name, I will do it.*
>
> John 14:13-14, NKJV

As a Substitution of Our Person:

The name of Jesus takes your place in prayer and also in ruling your world. He said:

> *And these signs will follow those who*
> *believe: in My name they will cast out*
> *demons.*   Mark 16:17, NKJV

> *Now John answered Him, saying,*
> *"Teacher, we saw someone who does not*
> *follow us casting out demons in Your*
> *name, and we forbade him because he*
> *does not follow us."*
> *But Jesus said, "Do not forbid him, for*
> *no one who works a miracle in My name*
> *can soon afterward speak evil of Me.*
>
> Mark 9:38-39, NKJV

Our dominion in life is impossible without the use of the name of Jesus:

> *The same followed Paul and us, and cried, saying, These men are the servants of the most high God, which shew unto us the way of salvation. And this did she many days. But Paul, being grieved, turned and said to the spirit, I command thee in the name of Jesus Christ to come out of her. And he came out the same hour.* Acts 16:17-18

As Authority:

The name of Jesus gives us authority in the three worlds:

> *Wherefore God also hath highly exalted him, and given him a name which is above every name: that at the name of Jesus every knee should bow, of things in heaven, and things in earth, and things under the earth;nd that every tongue should confess*

> *that Jesus Christ is Lord, to the glory of*
> *God the Father.*   Philippians 2:9-11

This doesn't happen automatically. We must walk in the consciousness of this fact. That is what brings the manifestation, not the magic of a name. When Jesus name is invoked in faith, He then exercises lordship over anything and everything.

It worked for the three Hebrew boys in the fire; they were able to rule that fire:

> *Then Nebuchadnezzar the king was astonished, and rose up in haste, and spake, and said unto his counsellors, Did not we cast three men bound into the midst of the fire?*
> *They answered and said unto the king, True, O king.*
> *He answered and said, Lo, I see four men loose, walking in the midst of the fire, and they have no hurt; and the form of the fourth is like the Son of God.*
> *Then Nebuchadnezzar came near to the mouth of the burning fiery furnace, and*

spake, and said, Shadrach, Meshach, and Abednego, ye servants of the most high God, come forth, and come hither. Then Shadrach, Meshach, and Abednego, came forth of the midst of the fire. And the princes, governors, and captains, and the king's counsellors, being gathered together, saw these men, upon whose bodies the fire had no power, nor was an hair of their head singed, neither were their coats changed, nor the smell of fire had passed on them.   Daniel 3:24-27

The Name Behind Every Miracle:

The utterance of the name of Jesus deploys supernatural manifestations of God:

And the seventy returned again with joy, saying, Lord, even the devils are subject unto us through thy name.
Luke 10:17

The sun shall be turned into darkness, and the moon into blood, before the great

189

> *and notable day of the Lord come: and*
> *it shall come to pass, that whosoever*
> *shall call on the name of the Lord shall*
> *be saved.* Acts 2:20-21

Miracles are meant to open doors and frustrate and put to rest the might and ability of both men and demons. Satan has his tricks, but God specializes in miracles. This was what finally humbled the mighty Pharaoh—the turning of Moses' rod into a serpent and back into a rod, the plagues that came upon Egypt, and the Israelites walking through the sea on dry ground. These were very special miracles.

In Jesus' time, it was the raising of the dead, the feeding of the five thousand, and many miraculous healings. These super-natural demonstrations performed by Jesus Christ can still be done today through the faith-filled use of His name.

The disciple of Jesus presented a dilemma for the first-century religious leaders:

What shall we do to these men? for that indeed a notable miracle hath been done by them is manifest to all them that dwell in Jerusalem; and we cannot deny it. But that it spread no further among the people, let us straitly threaten them, that they speak henceforth to no man in this name. Acts 4:16-17

It was clear to all that the notable miracles they were performing were only possible because of their use of Jesus' name.

Jesus was the fulfillment of Old Testament promises:

For Moses truly said unto the fathers, A prophet shall the Lord your God raise up unto you of your brethren, like unto me; him shall ye hear in all things whatsoever he shall say unto you. And it shall come to pass, that every soul, which will not hear that prophet, shall be destroyed from among the people. Acts 3:22-23

Without Jesus, we who are Gentiles are cut off from the covenant. But take up His name, and you can dominate your world. No wonder the Scriptures say:

> *And whatsoever ye do in word or deed, do all in the name of the Lord Jesus, giving thanks to God and the Father by him.* Colossians 3:17

Oh, how I love calling upon the matchless name of Jesus. Through that name, we have His endorsement, and therefore, anything can happen. Open your mouth right now and utilize the power and authority that come with the use of this name which is above every other name. Take charge of your circumstances in and through the name of Jesus.

Father, in the name of Jesus Christ, I remove from my life whatever is contrary to glory and virtue. Hindrances, get out of my way now in Jesus' mighty name!

Father, in the name of Jesus Christ, I decree a release right now of all that I need to manifest the fullness of Your blessings.

Now, you use that name and see what God will do for you.

Yes, we are *Joint Heirs with Christ* and, because of it, the world will see that we are different.

CHAPTER 14

THE GREAT SHIFT

And the seventh angel sounded; and there were great voices in heaven, saying, The kingdoms of this world are become the kingdoms of our Lord, and of his Christ; and he shall reign for ever and ever. Revelation 11:15

When Jesus Christ rose from the dead, there was a massive shift in the governance of this world. Suddenly, the ownership and rulership changed. Satan no longer ruled here anymore ... unless he was permitted to do so. The kingdom of this world become the Kingdom of our God and His Christ, and that transfer of power is permanent. *"He shall reign for ever and ever!"*

Now, for those who trust God and know how to utilize the name of Jesus Christ, the world is filled with peace, joy, righteousness, power, strength, honor and riches. God's preeminence on earth has been reestablished, and it was done in and through the name of Jesus Christ:

> *And being found in fashion as a man, he humbled himself, and became obedient unto death, even the death of the cross. Wherefore God also hath highly exalted him, and given him a name which is above every name: that at the name of Jesus every knee should bow, of things in heaven, and things in earth, and things under the earth; and that every tongue should confess that Jesus Christ is Lord, to the glory of God the Father.* Philippians 2:8-11

All the greatness of God is in the name of Jesus Christ:

> *The Father loveth the Son, and hath given all things into his hand. He that*

believeth on the Son hath everlasting life: and he that believeth not the Son shall not see life; but the wrath of God abideth on him. John 3:35-36

The operation of God is now in and through Jesus Christ:

Hath in these last days spoken unto us by his Son, whom he hath appointed heir of all things, by whom also he made the worlds; who being the brightness of his glory, and the express image of his person, and upholding all things by the word of his power, when he had by himself purged our sins, sat down on the right hand of the Majesty on high. Hebrews 1:2-3

God chose to demonstrate His love for us through His only begotten Son:

In this was manifested the love of God toward us, because that God sent his only begotten Son into the world, that we might live through him. 1 John 4:9

And again, when he bringeth in the firstbegotten into the world, he saith, And let all the angels of God worship him. Hebrews 1:6

The authority vested in the name of Jesus is the source of any and all of the mighty works done through the early Church. His name has been given to us as a tool for daily living and for dominion:

And whatsoever ye shall ask in my name, that will I do, that the Father may be glorified in the Son. If ye shall ask any thing in my name, I will do it.
John 14:13-14

Whatever you do, don't dare to doubt the ability that is to be found in the name of Jesus Christ. He said:

Believe me that I am in the Father, and the Father in me: or else believe me for the very works' sake. John 14:11

197

Jesus saith unto him, Have I been so long time with you, and yet hast thou not known me, Philip? he that hath seen me hath seen the Father; and how sayest thou then, Show us the Father?

John 14:9

I and my Father are one.   John 10:30

What Jesus Christ is is what His name is, and that is who Father God is. God raised Jesus from the dead, and now He is seated in the most powerful seat in the entire Universe, and His name controls everything:

And what is the exceeding greatness of his power to us-ward who believe, according to the working of his mighty power, which he wrought in Christ, when he raised him from the dead, and set him at his own right hand in the heavenly places, far above all principality, and power, and might, and dominion, and every name that is named, not only in this world, but also

198

in that which is to come: and hath put
all things under his feet, and gave him to
be the head over all things to the church.
Ephesians 1:19-22

The investment of God Almighty in the name makes it powerful, but the Church has yet to understand that our rulership on earth has been cemented by the authority God invested in that name.

Early in his Christian walk, Peter experienced the power of that name:

Then Peter said, Silver and gold
have I none; but such as I have give
I thee: In the name of Jesus Christ of
Nazareth rise up and walk. And he
took him by the right hand, and lifted
him up: and immediately his feet and
ankle bones received strength. And
he leaping up stood, and walked, and
entered with them into the temple,
walking, and leaping, and praising
God. Acts 3:6-8

The man was healed in and through the name of Jesus. There was nothing to be added. The moment Peter demanded the healing through the name of Jesus, the lame man started walking. Now, it's your turn to see wonders by learning to utilize in faith the name of Jesus Christ. Everything is designed to honor and obey that name:

> *And whatsoever ye do in word or deed, do all in the name of the Lord Jesus, giving thanks to God and the Father by him.* Colossians 3 :17

The early disciples were taught to do everything in that name, even to the giving of thanks:

> *Giving thanks always for all things unto God and the Father in the name of our Lord Jesus Christ.* Ephesians 5:20

According to 1 Corinthians, believers in Christ are washed, sanctified, and justified in and through the name of Jesus:

And such were some of you: but ye are washed, but ye are sanctified, but ye are justified in the name of the Lord Jesus, and by the Spirit of our God.
1 Corinthians 6:11

According to Hebrews, praising the name of Jesus is deemed a sacrifice unto God:

By him therefore let us offer the sacrifice of praise to God continually, that is, the fruit of our lips giving thanks to his name. Hebrews 13:15

Sacrifice has long been the most approved way of pleasing God, a way of connecting with His mercy. Every time the people of Israel made a sacrifice according to God's instructions, they experienced His divine intervention:

And Samuel took a sucking lamb, and offered it for a burnt offering wholly unto the Lord: and Samuel cried unto the Lord for Israel; and the Lord heard

201

> *him. And as Samuel was offering up*
> *the burnt offering, the Philistines drew*
> *near to battle against Israel: but the*
> *LORD thundered with a great thunder*
> *on that day upon the Philistines, and*
> *discomfited them; and they were smitten*
> *before Israel.* 1 Samuel 7:9-10

In David's day, a plague that had hindered the people of Israel stopped when he made a sacrifice at the threshing floor of Araunah:

> *And David built there an altar unto*
> *the LORD, and offered burnt offerings*
> *and peace offerings. So the LORD was*
> *intreated for the land, and the plague*
> *was stayed from Israel.*
> 2 Samuel 24:25

In olden days, a sacrifice meant butchering a prized animal and giving it to God upon an altar. Today the praise from your lips in the name of His Son is the sacrifice God desires.

According to 1 John, we are commanded to believe in the name of God's Son, Jesus Christ, and to love one another, even as He also commanded:

> *And this is his commandment, That we should believe on the name of his Son Jesus Christ, and love one another, as he gave us commandment. And he that keepeth his commandments dwelleth in him, and he in him. And hereby we know that he abideth in us, by the Spirit which he hath given us.* 1 John 3:23-24

"This is his [the Father's] commandment." According to Matthew, the divine presence comes by gathering together in Jesus' name:

> *For where two or three are gathered together in my [Jesus'] name, there am I in the midst of them.* Matthew 18:20

What a powerful name that it can command the divine presence.

According to James, we are to conquer sickness and disease by and through the name of Jesus:

> *Is any sick among you? let him call for the elders of the church; and let them pray over him, anointing him with oil in the name of the Lord: and the prayer of faith shall save the sick, and the Lord shall raise him up; and if he have committed sins, they shall be forgiven him.* James 5:14-15

Father, in the name of Jesus Christ, I open the door of opportunity for me and my family right now. Let helpers of destiny show up for us, Lord

Father, in the name of Jesus Christ, I demand every frustration and oppression around me to be removed, never to show up again

Father, in the name of Jesus Christ, whatever the enemy wants to use to fill my mind against my will, I cut off now.

Now, you use that name and see what God will do for you.

Yes, we are *Joint Heirs with Christ* and, because of it, the world will see that we are different.

CHAPTER 15

EVERY PROVISION IS TO BE FOUND IN HIS NAME

And blessed is she that believed: for there shall be a performance of those things which were told her from the Lord. Luke 1:45

Every provision of the Kingdom is deliverable on the platform of faith and in the name of Jesus Christ. *"Blessed is she that believed."* Performance follows your faith. It is not necessarily what we might think of as "a big faith"; it is faith in what God has said, a simple faith.

Jesus said to a group of blind men, *"According to your faith be it unto you"*:

And when he was come into the house, the blind men came to him: and Jesus saith unto them, Believe ye that I am able to do this?
They said unto him, Yea, Lord.
Then touched he their eyes, saying, According to your faith be it unto you. And their eyes were opened; and Jesus straitly charged them, saying, See that no man know it. Matthew 9:28-30

God is not limited; we're the limited ones because of our unbelief. Too often our faith is limited. Peter declared, *"And his [Jesus'] name through faith in his name hath made this man strong":*

And his name through faith in his name hath made this man strong, whom ye see and know: yea, the faith which is by him hath given him this perfect soundness in the presence of you all. Acts 3:16

Every generation has been given a tool of operation that made it unique, a representation of the King of Glory and an instrument of dominion on earth. For example, the ark of Noah ruled the flood. The water rose so high it covered the mountains and hills, but no matter how fierce death, lack, and destruction were, the devastation could not enter the ark. Noah and his family were safe. God was in that ark, and He had shut the door to the unbelieving.

The rod of Moses was an instrument of rulership, and it conquered the whole of Egypt and all her gods.

Fast forward to today, and the name of Jesus Christ has been given to the Church as a powerful instrument of operation. Nothing can stand against that name, and no one can overcome it:

> *And these signs shall follow them that believe; In my name shall they cast out devils; they shall speak with new tongues; they shall take up serpents; and if they drink any deadly thing, it shall not hurt them.*   Mark 16:17-18

As noted, the apostles saw this name at work at the beautiful gate:

> *Then Peter said, Silver and gold have I none; but such as I have give I thee: In the name of Jesus Christ of Nazareth rise* up and walk.　　　　　　Acts 3:6

The name of Jesus Christ—that was what God gave them to rule their world. It was a tenable force, a garment of power, and since then, every believer must wear it in order to dominate their world. *"In my name shall they cast out devils."* Why? Because the power and authority in the Person of Jesus is in His name and it rules over all:

> *And being found in fashion as a man, he humbled himself, and became obedient unto death, even the death of the cross. Wherefore God also hath highly exalted him, and given him a name which is above every name: that at the name of Jesus every knee should bow, of things in*

*heaven, and things in earth, and things
under the earth.*   Philippians 2:8-10

God shows up when the name of Jesus is spoken in faith, and mighty wonders are wrought in that name:

*And with great power gave the apostles
witness of the resurrection of the Lord
Jesus: and great grace was upon them
all.*   Act 4:33

Until religious people high-jacked the truth from the Church, miracles were its identity. Believers were sign carriers. Let's see it again:

*And these signs shall follow them that
believe; In my name shall they cast
out devils; they shall speak with new
tongues; they shall take up serpents; and
if they drink any deadly thing, it shall
not hurt them; they shall lay hands on
the sick, and they shall recover.*
                          Mark 16:17-18

The early believers *"turned the world upside down":*

> *And when they found them not, they drew Jason and certain brethren unto the rulers of the city, crying, These that have turned the world upside down are come hither also;* Acts 17:6

Why? Because *"notable,"* undeniable miracles were being performed in the name of Jesus:

> *What shall we do to these men? for that indeed a notable miracle hath been done by them is manifest to all them that dwell in Jerusalem; and we cannot deny it.* Acts 4:16

The conclusion was that they somehow had to make these people stop using the name of Jesus:

> *But that it spread no further among the people, let us straitly threaten them, that*

> *they speak henceforth to no man in this*
> *name.*   Acts 4:17

There is a difference between praying to God to receive something and using the authority in the name of Jesus to get results. Jesus clearly taught His disciples that when there was a need, they should go to the Father in Jesus' name:

> *And whatsoever ye shall ask in my*
> *name, that will I do, that the Father may*
> *be glorified in the Son.*   John 14:13

> *Ye have not chosen me, but I have chosen*
> *you, and ordained you, that ye should*
> *go and bring forth fruit, and that your*
> *fruit should remain: that whatsoever ye*
> *shall ask of the Father in my name, he*
> *may give it you.*   John 15:16

> *Verily, verily, I say unto you, Whatsoever*
> *ye shall ask the Father in my name, he*
> *will give it you.*   John 16:23

"Whatsoever you ask the father in my name, He will do it." Wow! What a promise! From this we understand that we are not to pray directly to Jesus; we are to pray to the Father in the name of Jesus.

Taking authority and dominion over an issue in the name of Jesus, however, is not a prayer. It is taking dominion, and we see the early disciples doing it often. At the beautiful gate, for instance, Peter and his companions didn't pray. They used the name of Jesus to invoke healing.

When Peter spoke to Aeneas, it was with the authority of the name of Jesus. It was not a prayer:

> *And there he found a certain man named Aeneas, which had kept his bed eight years, and was sick of the palsy. And Peter said unto him, Aeneas, Jesus Christ maketh thee whole: arise, and make thy bed. And he arose immediately.* Acts 9:33-34

Yes, in Acts 3, the disciples were on their way to the Temple to pray, but their ministry to the crippled man was not a prayer.

Paul arrested a foul spirit by merely using the name of Jesus. He didn't pray:

> *And it came to pass, as we went to prayer, a certain damsel possessed with a spirit of divination met us, which brought her masters much gain by soothsaying: the same followed Paul and us, and cried, saying, These men are the servants of the most high God, which shew unto us the way of salvation. And this did she many days. But Paul, being grieved, turned and said to the spirit, I command thee in the name of Jesus Christ to come out of her. And he came out the same hour.*
>
> Acts 16:16-18

Prayer is essential, but when we are confronted by demon spirits, we are to take authority over them in Jesus' name and command their obedience.

There is something in man that craves the miraculous. It excites him and he feels fulfilled by it. He knows it is supernatural, and he wants to be part of it. That human craving was honored by God when He gave us the power and authority of the name of Jesus Christ:

> *And now, Lord, behold their threaten-ings: and grant unto thy servants, that with all boldness they may speak thy word, by stretching forth thine hand to heal; and that signs and wonders may be done by the name of thy holy child Jesus.* Acts 4:29-30

Remember, Adam was the son of God and had his Father's nature and likeness ... that is, until sin came. God lost him in the garden, but He got him back in and through Christ, and man got back all that was lost and more.

The giving of the power of attorney to use the name of Jesus Christ was intended to separate us from the world and make it obvious who was the true God and who was the false. Remember Elijah and the prophets of Baal?

The Scriptures declare:

> *For in Him dwells all the fullness of the Godhead bodily.*
> Colossians 2:9, NKJV

Until now, we have not yet understood the greatness of God's power and glory, the immeasurable blessing that is in God, the Creator of the whole Universe, the One who can make something from nothing. He needed no raw materials to make the world and all that is in it appear. And all the fullness of God and the Holy Spirit are invested in One, and His name is Jesus Christ.

Everything is deposited into His name, and you and I are baptized into that name.

Always remember, our assignment here is to preach the Kingdom of God and the name of Jesus Christ:

But when they believed Philip as he preached the things concerning the kingdom of God and the name of Jesus Christ, both men and women were baptized.   Acts 8:12, NKJV

The finished work of Christ on the cross is all wrapped up in the name of Jesus Christ. Everything that Jesus is and everything that Jesus did is contained in His name. That's why no devil or situation can stand in the face of a believer who knows how to use the name of Jesus.

An *"it is finished'* anointing is found in that name. This is why the Scriptures say:

Because of the savour of thy good ointments thy name is as ointment poured forth, therefore do the virgins love thee.   Song of Solomon 1:3

Don't be fooled by religion and tradition. God has programmed the fact that when a man and a woman meet conjugally, a pregnancy occurs. It is an unconscious act of faith. If you block the air flow into your lungs, you will die. It's part of the program. In the same way, when the Rapture occurs, we will all be able to fly. It's in the program. It's also in the program of God that when you call on the name of Jesus by faith, sickness bows, and doors open. It has been said:

> *And it shall come to pass, that whosoever shall call on the name of the Lord shall be saved.*   Acts 2:21

> *For whosoever shall call upon the name of the Lord shall be saved.* Romans 10:13

Father, in the name of Jesus Christ, I am breaking forth right now on the right hand and on the left.

Father, in Jesus' name I put a stop to all the works of darkness that are coming against me.

Now, you use that name and see what God will do for you.

Yes, we are *Joint Heirs with Christ* and, because of it, the world will see that we are different.

CHAPTER 16

WEALTH AND POWER RESIDE IN HIS NAME

But my God shall supply all your need according to his riches in glory by Christ Jesus. Philippians 4:19

Through Christ, God transfers wealth to His people, either by blessing the works of their hands beyond their normal input, by connecting them with great opportunities, or by giving them divine ideas that bring attention to them. All these things are the works of God through supernatural intervention, and they are done in and through the name of Jesus.

When you use the name of Jesus by faith, God causes important people to notice you. They cannot pretend that His blessing is not upon your life. It is obvious to everyone:

> *For thou shalt break forth on the right hand and on the left; and thy seed shall inherit the Gentiles, and make the desolate cities to be inhabited. Fear not; for thou shalt not be ashamed: neither be thou confounded; for thou shalt not be put to shame: for thou shalt forget the shame of thy youth, and shalt not remember the reproach of thy widowhood any more. For thy Maker is thine husband; the LORD of hosts is his name; and thy Redeemer the Holy One of Israel; The God of the whole earth shall he be called.* Isaiah 54:3-5

Through the name of Jesus Christ, we gain access to all that God is and to the authority of His Kingdom. And His Kingdom rules over all:

> *The* LORD *hath prepared his throne in the heavens; and his kingdom ruleth over all.* Psalm 103:19

All demonic forces bow to the name of Jesus because He conquered them at His resurrection:

> *Blotting out the handwriting of ordinances that was against us, which was contrary to us, and took it out of the way, nailing it to his cross; and having spoiled principalities and powers, he made a shew of them openly, triumphing over them in it.* Colossians 2:14-15

> *Forasmuch then as the children are partakers of flesh and blood, he also himself likewise took part of the same; that through death he might destroy him that had the power of death, that is, the devil; and deliver them who through fear of death were all their lifetime subject to bondage.* Hebrews 2:14-15

There is a guarantee of results when we learn to use the name of Jesus in faith:

And whatsoever ye shall ask in my name, that will I do, that the Father may be glorified in the Son. If ye shall ask any thing in my name, I will do it.

John 14:13-14

Who could ask for a better guarantee than that?

In times of war, people look for safety, a place to hide, a place of protection. Jesus' name is our protection from the arrows of the wicked one. It's a strong tower in which we can safely hide. Today, we would call it our "bunker":

The name of the LORD is a strong tower: the righteous runneth into it, and is safe. Proverbs 18:10

The enemy has a hold on the old nature of man, but he has no authority over the new man? Why? Because he is a new creature

Joint Heirs with Christ

in Christ Jesus. This new man is under the law of life in Christ Jesus, not under the Law of sin and death. This prevents evil from entering your territory. There is an anointing upon the new man in Christ that breaks every yoke:

> *But if the Spirit of him that raised up Jesus from the dead dwell in you, he that raised up Christ from the dead shall also quicken your mortal bodies by his Spirit that dwelleth in you.* Romans 8:11

Your *"mortal body"* is your current body that carries the new man and is filled with the Holy Spirit. Because the body is mortal, the Holy Spirit dwells inside of it to *"quicken"* it or make it alive. In all of this, Satan has no authority to interfere. We are free:

> *There is therefore now no condemnation to them which are in Christ Jesus, who walk not after the flesh, but after the Spirit.* Romans 8:1

Those of us who are in Christ are completely free from the Law of sin and death, and that is the territory where the devil operates. Therefore, we are no longer under his government:

> *Who hath delivered us from the power of darkness, and hath translated us into the kingdom of his dear Son.*
> Colossians 1:13

When we permit the enemy to operate in our lives, we are allowing him to be bigger than he really is and to do more than he is lawfully allowed to do. The biblical command to the redeemed is to give him no space whatsoever:

> *And do not give the devil an opportunity [to lead you into sin by holding a grudge, or nurturing anger, or harboring resentment, or cultivating bitterness].*   Ephesians 4:27, AMP

The legality of our dominion is based on knowing that Jesus Christ bore our sins on the cross, and that goes a long way to affect the issue of sickness and disease, provisions for life and victory to live it in joy. Jesus took upon Himself cancer and diabetes, as well as our lack and poverty:

> *He personally carried our sins*
>   *in his body on the cross*
> *so that we can be dead to sin*
>   *and live for what is right.*
> *By his wounds*
>   *you are healed.*   1 Peter 2:24, NLT

The sin Jesus bore took care of all sickness and disease. Many believers in Christ agree that we can be free from sin because He took our sins upon Himself, but far fewer believe that He has also taken our sicknesses. They would rather believe their symptoms. But just as my sins are forgiven, my sickness is also healed:

Jesus climbed into a boat and went back across the lake to his own town. Some people brought to him a paralyzed man on a mat. Seeing their faith, Jesus said to the paralyzed man, "Be encouraged, my child! Your sins are forgiven."

But some of the teachers of religious law said to themselves, "That's blasphemy! Does he think he's God?"

Jesus knew what they were thinking, so he asked them, "Why do you have such evil thoughts in your hearts? Is it easier to say 'Your sins are forgiven,' or 'Stand up and walk'? So I will prove to you that the Son of Man has the authority on earth to forgive sins." Then Jesus turned to the paralyzed man and said, "Stand up, pick up your mat, and go home!"

And the man jumped up and went home! Matthew 9:1-7, NLT

He canceled the record of the charges against us and took it away by nailing it to the cross. In this way, he disarmed the spiritual rulers and authorities. He

shamed them publicly by his victory
over them on the cross.
Colossians 2:14-15, NLT

Is this true in your life? If not, establish it today in and through the name of Jesus Christ.

Being saved doesn't mean joining a religion; it means putting on Christ and taking up the power and authority of His name:

This means that anyone who belongs to
Christ has become a new person. The old
life is gone; a new life has begun!
2 Corinthians 5:17, NLT

For as many of you as have been bap-
tized into Christ have put on Christ.
Galatians 3:27

And have put on the new man, which is
renewed in knowledge after the image
of him that created him.
Colossians 3:10

Being in Christ and having access to His name is the safest place in the Universe. He is our Eden. And in Eden enemy access is forbidden. Therefore, when the enemy tries to use his tricks against us, we need to stand our ground based on the finished work of Christ. We must declare, "Satan, this is beyond your reach. You have no authority here, so you can't touch me. You are forbidden entry here. I am in Christ, and therefore I am far above you."

Defend your territory, and have no pending issues with the enemy.

Jesus said to John:

> *I am he that liveth, and was dead; and, behold, I am alive for evermore, Amen; and have the keys of hell and of death. Write the things which thou hast seen, and the things which are, and the things which shall be hereafter.* Revelation 1:18-19

It's already done. Jesus performed His heavenly assignment perfectly, and we are now the beneficiaries through His name:

And she shall bring forth a son, and thou shalt call his name Jesus: for he shall save his people from their sins .   Matthew 1:21

Therefore the LORD *himself shall give you a sign; Behold, a virgin shall conceive, and bear a son, and shall call his name Immanuel.*   Isaiah 7:14

Immanuel (or Emmanuel) means *"God with us"*:

Behold, a virgin shall be with child, and shall bring forth a son, and they shall call his name Emmanuel, which being interpreted is, God with us.
                      Matthew 1:23

For where two or three are gathered together in my name, there am I in the midst of them.   Matthew 18:20

We who are believers in Christ are to cause a commotion in the Kingdom of darkness by demonstrating the power that resides in us in and through the name of Jesus.

The Jewish religious leaders of the first century questioned Jesus' disciples about whose name they used:

> *And when they had set them in the midst, they asked, By what power, or by what name, have ye done this?*
>
> Acts 4:7

That generation saw something great in the name being used, and this must be the identity of the Church today, not noise, but wonders in and through the name of Jesus Christ. This was the experience of the disciples Jesus chose:

> *And the seventy returned again with joy, saying, Lord, even the devils are subject unto us through thy name.*
>
> Luke 10:17

When we believe and utilize the authority and power of the name given to us, power erupts, and God receives all the glory:

But as many as received him, to them gave he power to become the sons of God, even to them that believe on his name. John 1:12

Establishing the power and authority of Jesus' name was at the core of His earthly assignment:

Now when he was in Jerusalem at the passover, in the feast day, many believed in his name, when they saw the miracles which he did. John 2:23

His name brought wonders, and the people who witnessed those wonders then believed in His name.

Now, you use that name and see what God will do for you.

Yes, we are *Joint Heirs with Christ* and, because of it, the world will see that we are different.

CHAPTER 17

Everything We Do Must Be Done in Jesus' Name

And whatever you do in word or deed, do all in the name of the Lord Jesus, giving thanks to God the Father through Him. Colossians 3:17, NKJV

"Whatever you do in word or deed." That's everything. We are to use the name of Jesus in literally everything we do.

It is through His name that salvation comes:

He that believeth on him is not condemned: but he that believeth not is condemned already, because he hath not believed in the name of the only begotten Son of God. John 3:18

After we believe, we are to be baptized into His name:

> *Go ye therefore, and teach all nations, baptizing them in the name of the Father, and of the Son, and of the Holy Ghost.*   Matthew 28:19

It is through His name that we have access to the Father:

> *Ye have not chosen me, but I have chosen you, and ordained you, that ye should go and bring forth fruit, and that your fruit should remain: that whatsoever ye shall ask of the Father in my name, he may give it you.*   John 15:16

Jesus is now seated at the right hand of God, and He says, "Your petition has been granted." He has such a high standing in Heaven that no one who calls on the Father through His name can be denied. What an assurance! Why would we ever hesitate to use that name?

There must be no stagnation in your life. Jesus has destined you to excel at all you do and say, but in order to achieve that, everything must be done in His name and for His glory.

The early disciples of Jesus were simple people, and yet they excelled everywhere they went:

> *And through the hands of the apostles many signs and wonders were done among the people.* Acts 5:12

The fact that you have such power and authority threatens and intimidates the enemy:

> *"But so that it spreads no further among the people, let us severely threaten them, that from now on they speak to no man in this name." So they called them and commanded them not to speak at all nor teach in the name of Jesus.*
> *But Peter and John answered and said to them, "Whether it is right in the sight of God to listen to you more than to God, you judge."* Acts 4:17-19, NKJV

The name of Jesus stirs judgement upon the wicked and eliminates their hold:

> *"Did we not strictly command you not to teach in this name? And look, you have filled Jerusalem with your doctrine, and intend to bring this Man's blood on us!"* Acts 5:28, NKJV

Because Satan hates Jesus, he also hates you and will do anything he can to hinder you:

> *Therefore we wanted to come to you — even I, Paul, time and again — but Satan hindered us.*
> 1 Thessalonians 2:18, NKJV

Declare with me today:

Every power working behind the scenes to frustrate my efforts and plans is scattered and destroyed now in the name of Jesus Christ! Amen!

The early believers were persecuted for their faith:

> *And the night following the Lord stood by him, and said, Be of good cheer, Paul: for as thou hast testified of me in Jerusalem, so must thou bear witness also at Rome. And when it was day, certain of the Jews banded together, and bound themselves under a curse, saying that they would neither eat nor drink till they had killed Paul.*   Acts 23:11-19

Let us declare:

Every deception of the enemy is exposed now and nullified in my life!

The Lord will faithfully expose Satan's plans:

> *Then the Spirit lifted me and brought me to the east gateway of the LORD's Temple, where I saw twenty-five prominent men of the city. Among them were*

Jaazaniah son of Azzur and Pelatiah son of Benaiah, who were leaders among the people. The Spirit said to me, "Son of man, these are the men who are planning evil and giving wicked counsel in this city. They say to the people, 'Is it not a good time to build houses? This city is like an iron pot. We are safe inside it like meat in a pot.' Therefore, son of man, prophesy against them loudly and clearly."   Ezekiel 11:1-4, NLT

God has your back, and you can overcome anything and every thing in Jesus' name:

"Therefore, this is what the Sovereign LORD says: This city is an iron pot all right, but the pieces of meat are the victims of your injustice. As for you, I will soon drag you from this pot. I will bring on you the sword of war you so greatly fear, says the Sovereign LORD. I will drive you out of Jerusalem and hand you over to foreigners, who will carry out my judgments against you.

You will be slaughtered all the way to the borders of Israel. I will execute judgment on you, and you will know that I am the LORD. No, this city will not be an iron pot for you, and you will not be like meat safe inside it. I will judge you even to the borders of Israel, and you will know that I am the LORD. For you have refused to obey my decrees and regulations; instead, you have copied the standards of the nations around you."

Ezekiel 11:7-12, NLT

Declare even now:

Every evil counsel against my life, my family, and my church, is exposed and defeated in the name of Jesus Christ!

God said, *"Prophesy against them."* So, do it, and do it now!

I silence every trouble and decree peace all around me in the days ahead in Jesus' name!

Forasmuch then as the children are partakers of flesh and blood, he also himself likewise took part of the same; that through death he might destroy him that had the power of death, that is, the devil; And deliver them who through fear of death were all their lifetime subject to bondage. Hebrews 2:14-15

Boldly delare:

Death and fear, your power is destroyed now in my life, my home, and my children in Jesus' name and for His glory.

Through a divine order, God has given us the name of Jesus Christ as our instrument to rule the world. All that Adam lost in the garden is coming back to us now through that matchless name, Jesus Christ:

Wherefore God also hath highly exalted him, and given him a name which is above every name: that at the name of Jesus every knee should bow, of things

in heaven, and things in earth, and things under the earth; and that every tongue should confess that Jesus Christ is Lord, to the glory of God the Father.
Philippians 2:9-11

We are not at the mercy of anyone or anything in this Universe. Declare today:

Every being, you must bow to the name of Jesus Christ, and that name is our possession. Yokes must be broken, and the oppressed must go free right now in Jesus' name.

The name of Jesus Christ, the name above every other name, is the key to our dominion. Our confidence is boosted to face every conceivable situation by that name. Through it, power is released for performance:

But as many as received him, to them gave he power to become the sons of God, even to them that believe on his name.
John 1:12

Now, you use that name and see what God will do for you.

Yes, we are *Joint Heirs with Christ* and, because of it, the world will see that we are different.

CHAPTER 18

RULED BY THE SPIRIT

*For as many as are led by the Spirit of
God, they are the sons of God.*

Romans 8:14

In order to rule your world through the
name of Jesus, you must allow God's Spirit
to rule your mind and heart. When sense
knowledge takes over the reality of the
truth, our dominion is lost. But we are born
of the Spirit, made in the image of the living
God. Therefore, we are not to be governed
by our senses, but by the Spirit. Then our
senses will follow.

Jesus said:

> *It is the spirit that quickeneth; the flesh profiteth nothing: the words that I speak unto you, they are spirit, and they are life.* John 6:63

We must believe the Word of God and not our experiences. Thank God for your feelings, emotions, and thoughts, but they are not to rule you. Your senses pick up information from the physical world, not from the realm of the Spirit.

Jesus said very clearly:

> *It is written, Man shall not live by bread alone, but by every word that proceedeth out of the mouth of God.* Matthew 4:4

When the average believer experiences the physical symptoms of sickness, they quickly come to the conclusion that they are not healed, even though God's Word says they are. God said, *"They shall recover"*:

> *And these signs shall follow them that believe; In my name shall they cast*

out devils; they shall speak with new tongues; they shall take up serpents; and if they drink any deadly thing, it shall not hurt them; they shall lay hands on the sick, and they shall recover.

Mark 16:17

God said, *"Ye were healed"*:

Who his own self bare our sins in his own body on the tree, that we, being dead to sins, should live unto righteousness: by whose stripes ye were healed.

1 Peter 2:24

How? In the power and authority of the name of Jesus Christ. Learn to use that name and then say what the Word says:

By His stripes, I am whole.
I am healed in Jesus' name.

Say it in faith and use the name of authority, and it will manifest.

**I am blessed in the name of Jesus Christ.
I am rich in the name of Jesus Christ.**

As we make these declarations of faith and seal them with the name we have been given as key to heavenly access, we are giving the High Priest of our confession something to work with. And He never fails!

There is something about the name of Jesus Christ that goes far beyond religion. The entire Universe recognizes it. That name is honored, not only in Heaven, but also on earth and under the earth.

It worked for Philip:

> *But when they believed Philip preaching the things concerning the kingdom of God, and the name of Jesus Christ, they were baptized, both men and women.*
>
> Acts 8:12

When Paul was converted, His assignment was about the name of Jesus. He was to take it everywhere. And it was not just for preaching and teaching. God

246

was in that name, and that name would work wonders:

> *But the Lord said unto him, Go thy way: for he is a chosen vessel unto me, to bear my name before the Gentiles, and kings, and the children of Israel: for I will shew him how great things he must suffer for my name's sake.* Acts 9:15-16

This name was and is a tool for the rescue of humanity. It is a strong tower for anyone who needs help. That is what Paul was sent to preach:

> *But Barnabas took him, and brought him to the apostles, and declared unto them how he had seen the Lord in the way, and that he had spoken to him, and how he had preached boldly at Damascus in the name of Jesus.*
> *And he was with them coming in and going out at Jerusalem. And he spake boldly in the name of the Lord Jesus, and disputed against the Grecians: but they went about to slay him.* Acts 9:27-29

Using the name of Jesus worked for Philip in Samaria, and he took the city by storm:

> *Then Philip went down to the city of Samaria, and preached Christ unto them. And the people with one accord gave heed unto those things which Philip spake, hearing and seeing the miracles which he did. For unclean spirits, crying with loud voice, came out of many that were possessed with them: and many taken with palsies, and that were lame, were healed. And there was great joy in that city.* Acts 8:5-8

Unlimited joy is your portion now. If things are not the way you want them, take authority over your situation in Jesus' name. We are called and destined *"for his name"*:

> *Simeon hath declared how God at the first did visit the Gentiles, to take out of them a people for his name.*
>
> Acts 15:14

We are Jesus people. He is our identity, and we are called unto His name:

> *Unto the church of God which is at Corinth, to them that are sanctified in Christ Jesus, called to be saints, with all that in every place call upon the name of Jesus Christ our Lord, both theirs and ours: Grace be unto you, and peace, from God our Father, and from the Lord Jesus Christ.* 1 Corinthians 1:2-3

Our full identity, as believers and children of God, is in the name of Jesus. It is our standard. That name is the source of strength and encouragement to the Church. The Bible says:

> *And whatsoever ye do in word or deed, do all in the name of the Lord Jesus, giving thanks to God and the Father by him.* Colossians 3:17

> *In the name of our Lord Jesus Christ, when ye are gathered together, and my*

spirit, with the power of our Lord Jesus Christ ... .   1 Corinthians 5:4

For where two or three are gathered together in my name, there am I in the midst of them.   Matthew 18:20

Yes, even our gathering together is to be done in the name of Jesus Christ. We are washed, sanctified, and justified in that precious name:

And such were some of you: but ye are washed, but ye are sanctified, but ye are justified in the name of the Lord Jesus, and by the Spirit of our God.
1 Corinthians 6:11

And we give God the Father thanks in that name:

Giving thanks always for all things unto God and the Father in the name of our Lord Jesus Christ.   Ephesians 5:20

Everywhere that name is honored, God is glorified and His power manifest. In Him all things consist:

> *For by him were all things created, that are in heaven, and that are in earth, visible and invisible, whether they be thrones, or dominions, or principalities, or powers: all things were created by him, and for him: and he is before all things, and by him all things consist. And he is the head of the body, the church: who is the beginning, the firstborn from the dead; that in all things he might have the preeminence. For it pleased the Father that in him should all fulness dwell; and, having made peace through the blood of his cross, by him to reconcile all things unto himself; by him, I say, whether they be things in earth, or things in heaven.*
>
> Colossians 1:16-20

> *Wherefore also we pray always for you, that our God would count you worthy*

of this calling, and fulfil all the good pleasure of his goodness, and the work of faith with power: that the name of our Lord Jesus Christ may be glorified in you, and ye in him, according to the grace of our God and the Lord Jesus Christ. 2 Thessalonians 1:11-12

The early Church was powerful because the name of Jesus was honored. When any instruction is given in the name of Jesus Christ, that is the end of controversies:

By him therefore let us offer the sacrifice of praise to God continually, that is, the fruit of our lips giving thanks to his name. Hebrews 13:15

Is any sick among you? let him call for the elders of the church; and let them pray over him, anointing him with oil in the name of the Lord: and the prayer of faith shall save the sick, and the Lord shall raise him up; and if he have committed sins, they shall be forgiven him. James 5:14-15

Amazingly, today some who call themselves Christians prefer not to use the name of Jesus publicly. They are afraid it will offend someone:

> *If ye be reproached for the name of Christ, happy are ye; for the spirit of glory and of God resteth upon you: on their part he is evil spoken of, but on your part he is glorified.*   1 Peter 4:14

But this is an enemy tactic to stop the flow of power to the Church. Even our sins were forgiven for His name's sake:

> *I write unto you, little children, because your sins are forgiven you for his name's sake.*   1 John 2:12

This is much more than religious identification; it is a command. Everything is to be done in the name of Jesus Christ. Hallelujah! Everything!

When we ask God for something in Jesus' name, Jesus goes into action, and God is glorified. The world is about to witness a glory that is uncommon and results that are beyond description, and it will all be done in Jesus' name:

> *And whatsoever ye shall ask in my name, that will I do, that the Father may be glorified in the Son. If ye shall ask any thing in my name, I will do it.*
>
> John 14:13-14

"If ye shall ask any thing in my name, I will do it." All Jesus did in His death and resurrection is now applied through His name. When you use that name, the name of the Accomplisher of All Things, Heaven responds. That is the name of our Healer, the name of our Provider, the name of our Defender. All that He is is in that name.

So, stop acting and living as if Jesus died in vain. No! He is our Substitute, and whatever He died for we must never bear again.

He lives in Heaven as me, and I live on earth like Him.

Herein is our love made perfect, that we may have boldness in the day of judgment: because as he is, so are we in this world. 1 John 4:17

I am crucified with Christ: nevertheless I live; yet not I, but Christ liveth in me: and the life which I now live in the flesh I live by the faith of the Son of God, who loved me, and gave himself for me. Galatians 2:20

This is where we stand as believers in Jesus Christ, and it's a reality we need to absorb. God now is able to rule the earth through you and me and reign by the authority of His name spoken by our mouths. He gets all the honor and glory when we display His power through His name.

God's promise is:

Whosoever shall call on the name of the Lord shall be saved. Acts 2:21

255

So, what are you waiting for? Call on that name today. Claim your inheritance. You have God's permission and His authority to use His name and see what He will do for you and your family.

Yes, we are *Joint Heirs with Christ* and, because of it, the world will see that we are different.

OTHER BOOKS BY
DR. ABIOLA IDOWU

HEAVEN on EARTH

Bishop Dr. Abiola Idowu

WALKING
AND
LIVING
IN YOUR
INHERITANCE

BISHOP ABIOLA IDOWU

WEALTH
FAVOUR JOY
GOOD HEALTH
TRANSFORMATION

LIVING BY
ORIGINAL
DESIGN

IN
CHARGE

BISHOP ABIOLA IDOWU

RULING *Your* WORLD

DR. ABIOLA IDOWU

Dr. Abiola Idowu

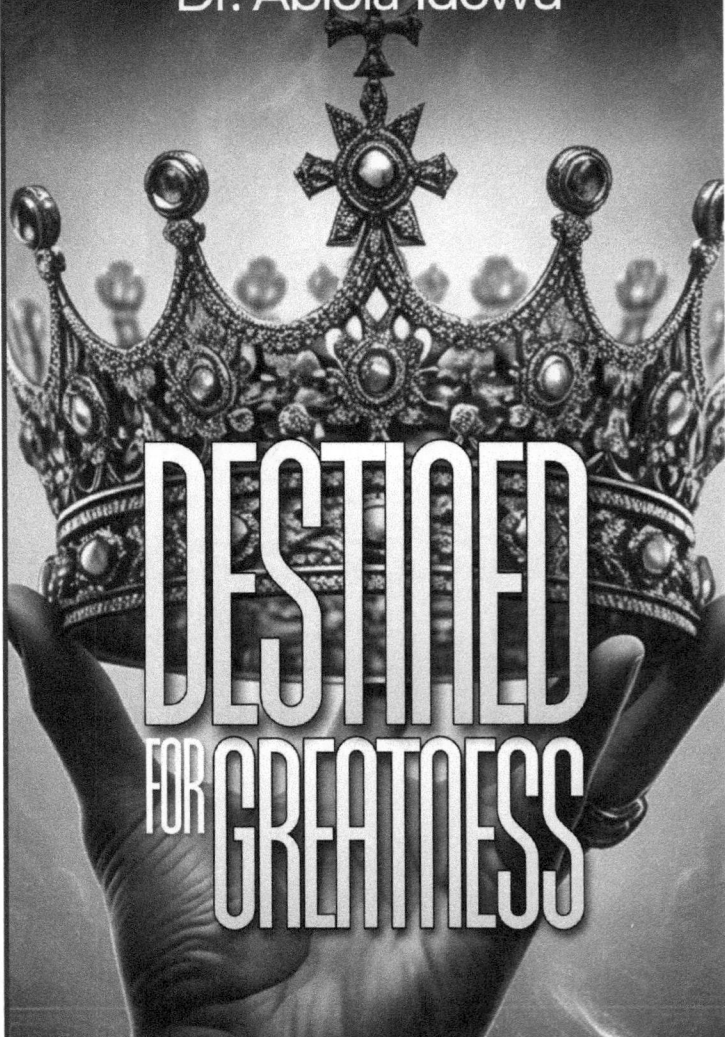

DESTINED FOR GREATNESS

OTHER BOOKS BY
DR. ABIOLA IDOWU

AUTHOR CONTACT INFORMATION

You may contact the author directly in the following way:

eMail: Bishopidowu@crepa.org

Telephone: (904) 469-5724